POPE JOHN PAUL II

POPE JOHN PAUL II

John Moody

A Balliett & Fitzgerald Book

A Literary Express, Inc. book
(a subsidiary of Doubleday Direct, Inc.)
Reprinted by special arrangement with:
Crown Publishers, Inc.
a division of Random House, Inc.
201 East 50th Street
New York, New York 10022

PRINTING HISTORY:

Park Lane Press/1997
Literary Express, Inc./1998

A&E and BIOGRAPHY are trademarks of A&E Television Networks,
registered in the United States and other countries.

A Balliett & Fitzgerald Book
Series Editor: Thomas Dyja
Book Design: Lisa Govan, Susan Canavan
Copy Editor: William Drennan
Photo Research: Maria Fernandez
and special thanks to Judy Capadanno, Bill Huelster,
and John Groton at Random House

If you would be interested in purchasing additional copies of this book,
please write to this address for information:

Biographyâ Bookshelf
1540 Broadway
New York, NY 10036

ISBN: 1-58165-047-7

Printed in the United States of America

CONTENTS

1921

CHAPTER ONE

CHURCH STREET

The main square of Wadowice, a drab industrial town thirty miles southwest of Kraków, is a gray-brown expanse where commerce and religion have coexisted all through the procession of modern Polish history. The newspaper kiosk commands a view of everything that happens here. The northern mouth of the square leads to an open-air market where merchants have peddled fruits and vegetables, soap and shoestrings, candies and condiments since the fourteenth century; today, their successors add lightbulbs, chewing gum, matchbooks, VCR tapes, computer discs, and other modern innovations to the array of products on display. The other end of the square, to the south, is devoted to the fulfillment of spiritual needs. The onion-domed Church of Our Lady of Perpetual Aid dominates not only the town's geographic center but also its social life. Posters outside announce music recitals, poetry readings, and prayer sessions that draw a cross section of Wadowice's twelve thousand residents.

Yet neither the church nor the dignified square on which it stands is Wadowice's leading tourist attraction. Though Wadowice considers its pure rural water supply a particular point of pride, the town has another, greater boast, one that draws tens of thousands of visitors every year to an unremarkable-looking apartment building that faces the west side of the house of worship, separated only by a narrow walkway known as Koscielna, or Church, Street. By normal tourist standards, No. 7 Church Street is less a monument than a monumental letdown. Once owned by a family of glass merchants and now the property of the municipal government, its architecture is indifferent, its state of repair haphazard, but every year 180,000 pilgrims troop up its iron-banistered stairway to the second floor, where they are greeted at the top by the stern visage of Sister Magdalena. She is the guide to this most holy place: two rooms and a kitchen with a yellow-tiled floor and wood-burning stove that keeps the apartment stiflingly warm on all but the coldest of days.

❧ ❧ ❧

"The Christ of Nations"

Inside, the flat is filled with glass-walled cases and roped-off exhibits that appear to be nothing more than the oddments of an active life—a pair of hickory skis, a can of downhill ski wax, camping equipment, a canoe paddle, a pair of cloudy sunglasses, all evidence that the chief benefactor and subject of this dusty, dated archive was for many years an avid sportsman. But the true devotion of Karol Józef Wojtyla, who was born in this humble abode on May 18, 1920, was to another goal—the glory of his God, whose vicar on earth he would become on October 16, 1978.

To comprehend the complex personality of Karol Wojtyla—Pope John Paul II—one must see more than just his home; one must understand the tortured history of his homeland and that of his family, both stories of faith in the face of evil and loss. As Poland survived through tragedy after tragedy—from its dissolution under the Austro-Hungarian Empire, to the horrors of anti-Semitic purges and Nazi Auschwitz, built just a few

The Wojtyla home in Wadowice, where young Karol was born.

THE FLAT PLACE

Perhaps it is Poland's resolute flatness that makes it so attractive to invaders. Three-quarters of the country is lowlands, and its Baltic coast is difficult to defend against determined marine assault. Moreover, the author of history mischievously set Poland among three aggressive empires—German, Russian, and Prussian—then settled back to see which would overwhelm its windy plains.

They took turns. After manipulating the German king Henry IV, who was engaged in a running dispute with Pope Gregory VII in the eleventh century, Poland's king Boleslaw II thought he had secured Polish independence from its neighbors. Boleslaw III then decided that the best way to keep Poland

from being divided among his enemies was to partition it between his sons. This had the predictable effect of creating animosity among the regions, and set Poland up for invasion. In 1240 Mongols overwhelmed the city of Kiev and held parts of Poland for another fifty years. From beyond the grave, St. Stanislaw, who was canonized in 1253, came to his homeland's rescue. His cult of followers helped bring Poland into the Holy Roman Empire and yoked the country's future securely to that of Western Europe.

By the fourteenth century, Poland was enjoying an era of peace and prosperity that its latter-day sons and daughters would view with longing. During the thirty-seven-year reign of King Kazimierz the Great, Polish arts and culture flourished. Kazimierz founded and provided the funding for Kraków University, and encouraged the development of dozens of cities and towns that strengthened the country's sense of identity. Finally, and most lastingly to his credit, Kazimierz turned Poland into a refuge for Jews fleeing persecution and pogroms from the rest of Europe, particularly in Russia and Germany. As the century came to its end, Poland found itself united with a traditional border foe, Lithuania, through the marriage of Crown Princess Jadwiga and Lithuania's king Jagiello, who took the name Wladyslaw II Jagiello when he assumed the throne of Poland. More importantly, Wladyslaw embraced the Christian faith, and pressed it upon his native land, ensuring that Poland and its neighbor would forever be aligned with the Christian traditions of the West.

Wladyslaw's son and successor, Wladyslaw III, formed an alliance with the bishop of Kraków, and used his military might to temporarily save Byzantium, the eastern capital of the Catholic Church now known as Istanbul, from assault by the Ottoman Empire. The Ottomans eventually swarmed the city, and for more than a century menaced Europe.

The Russian czar, Ivan III, took advantage of the situation to attack Lithuania; at the same time, Germany staged a rebellion against Polish rule in the Bohemian regions to the south. During this time, the power of the monarchy receded in favor of the country's nobility. These aristocrats used their new dominance to exploit the country's peasants and enrich themselves. At the same time, they encouraged the spread of education and culture. Polish manufactures and agriculture flourished. The Baltic port of Gdansk became a clearinghouse of European commerce. The influence of the Catholic Church was felt, too. Both the newly organized Protestant sects and the Eastern Orthodox Church were tolerated, but the Roman See clearly dominated.

In 1683 it was the military genius of Jan III Sobieski, then Poland's king, that relieved the Ottoman siege of Vienna. Ironically, by throwing back the Turkish threat, Poland's monarch helped make it possible for Russia and Austria to develop into strong empires; both would return the favor by harassing Poland in coming years.

Late in the eighteenth century, Catherine the Great used her minister in Warsaw to meddle in Polish affairs and agitate for better treatment for the country's non–Roman Catholic minorities. This led to fighting, which in turn drew Frederick II of Prussia to invade Poland. As a way of restoring peace, Russia, Austria, and Prussia in 1772 partitioned Poland–for the first time.

The country's division would be reworked twice more, in 1793 and 1795, always in favor of Russia, Prussia, and Austria, and remain in effect until 1914.

miles from Wojtyla's birthplace, to the totalitarian shadow of the Soviet Union, so did the Wojtylas suffer many blows, with only faith to carry them.

Wadowice, located in the breast of the Beskidy Mountains, was part of the Austro-Hungarian Empire until 1918, when the Versailles Treaty reversed the 123-year-long partition of Poland among Russia, Prussia, and Austria and re-created, for a short window of time, a sovereign state. Having maintained their Polish culture through the partition, Poles now united with a strong sense of patriotism. When Polish forces led by Marshal Josef Pilsudski repelled Soviet troops hoping to sweep westward into Germany in 1920, a battle known as the Miracle on the Vistula, Poland once again saw itself as the savior of the West. Polish nationalism surged, and it was during this first flowering of modern Poland that Karol Wojtyla was born and raised.

Along with Polish nationalism, Polish Catholicism also surged; it is impossible to speak of one without the other. The Polish nation and the Polish church were formed at the same moment in 966, the result of a marriage that allied a pagan tribe and a Bohemian Christian dynasty, making both nation and church fundamental to any understanding of Polish consciousness. Several great figures of Polish history have been canonized, such as St. Stanislaw, a bishop martyred in 1079 by King Boleslaw II for opposing his licentious reign, while others, such as Queen Jadwiga, a Polish ruler whose marriage created a large Polish-Lithuanian empire in 1386, have been beatified, the step prior to canonization. Poland's precarious placement between so many of history's empires has given it the role of gate between East and West, a role it chose when during the Schism of 1054 the Western Catholic Church, which looked to Rome for authority, and the Greek-dominated Orthodox Church, which looked to the East, broke apart and

Young Karol with his father, Lt. Karol Wojtyla, Sr.

Poland chose to adhere to the Western faith; since then it has been the first conquest of many invaders moving in either direction. An image of Poland as the "Christ of Nations," suffering to save the world, arose and is still promulgated by some today. Until early in the twentieth century, Latin remained the language of official business in Poland. As Wojtyla himself said when he returned to Poland for the first time as pope, "Through the course of history, Poland has been linked to the Church of Christ and the See of Rome by a special bond of spiritual unity. Without Christ it is impossible to understand the history of Poland."

By the standards of most small, East European towns, Wadowice in the early years of the twentieth century was set apart by its rich cultural life. Plays were regularly staged, libraries well attended, and the school was renowned for its faculty. Wadowice also had a small but financially influential Jewish population. Once welcomed in Poland by King Kazimierz the Great, Polish Jews found themselves the target of periodic purges, though less fierce than those that ravaged their neighbors in the Ukraine and Russia. Anti-Semitism had been a facet of Polish life for centuries, reaching its tragic zenith in the deportation and extermination of 3 million Polish Jews by the Nazis. The strong Jewish presence in Wadowice created if not harmony between members of the two religions, then at least a greater tolerance than often found elsewhere in the country.

Karol was the second son of a career army officer, also named Karol Wojtyla, and his wife, Emilia, who was five years younger than he. Both husband and wife were from Silesia, a region of Poland with mixed German and Polish ethnicity, though Emilia's upholsterer father had moved their family to Kraków when she was a year old. She had been educated in a convent as a child. The Wojtylas' elder boy, Edmund, had been born in 1906, the year the Wojtylas were married, followed by a daughter named

Olga, who died as an infant. The Wojtylas subsisted on a minuscule army salary, most of the elder Wojtyla's active duty being in the service of the Austrian Empire, which had ruled southern Poland. Though he had a good army record, Wojtyla was rising slowly up the ranks until Poland's independence in 1919 after World War I, when he was promoted to lieutenant in the 12th Regiment of the Polish Army, and moved to Wadowice from Kraków. Karol's mother, whose health was never robust, did piecework sewing to add to their income. The parents of both Karol, Sr., and Emilia died before young Karol was born.

The family was devoutly Catholic, possibly even more so than most in this nation bound so inextricably to the Church. Lieutenant Wojtyla carried a lifelong and unshakable faith that defined the family environment. His children were baptized by a military chaplain—young Karol on June 20, 1920, a month after his birth. Their apartment was dotted with pictures of saints and scenes from the New Testament. Each night, after dinner, the family Bible was opened, read aloud, and discussed. Both Karol—known by the diminutive Lolek (a name some of his earliest friends still used seventy years later to refer to him)—and his older brother, Edmund, inherited from their father a deep belief in the authority of the Church, its teachings, and its mysteries. The strength imparted by that faith would become the cornerstone of Karol Wojtyla's personality, and the basis upon which he has lived his extraordinary life.

Young Lolek's first encounter with tragedy took place on April 13, 1929, in his ninth year, when his mother succumbed at age forty-five to combined heart and kidney failure. Although those few childhood friends who remember his mother and her death recall that Karol maintained his composure far beyond what might be expected of a young boy, the untimely loss left its mark. In his later years as pope, he would sometimes make reference to motherhood and his own mother, usually with a mixture of openhearted love and regret in his voice. Though Wojtyla's easy traffic in the lay world would bring him many friends who were women, none would come closer to him than the woman who had just died. His lifelong devotion to the Virgin Mary was doubtless tied to his own sense of personal loss, as well as being a source of comfort.

With Edmund attending school in nearby Kraków, Lieutenant Wojtyla (who had retired from active service in 1928) and Karol were left alone in the second-floor apartment on Church Street. Their life together might have been a descent into melancholy, but instead they made it into a mutually fortifying quest for spiritual and intellectual fulfillment. They began to attend morning Mass together before school at the church across the street. During the day, the boy made steady progress through grammar school, while his father kept the apartment in order and prepared a small dinner for both of them. After homework and housework were completed, the two often ended their day with a casual stroll around town, followed by evening prayers. They were also known to play soccer in the half-empty flat, the parlor having been closed off after the death of Mrs. Wojtyla, this being now a house of only males. While the elder Wojtyla's army pension was barely adequate for their needs, in later years the pope remembered his childhood as one of plenty, not of penury. Clearly Wojtyla had taught his son well and early that man does not live by bread alone.

From his earliest years, Karol's range of interests and activities was astounding, perhaps as much because of the hardships and loneliness he had faced as in spite of them. He was a standout student at the grammar school, then housed in the same building as the municipal hall. The school had a notable faculty, and Karol achieved high grades as well as serving as an altar boy and playing on the school soccer team. He also read poetry at a precocious age; attended the theater, for which he developed a lifelong passion; and excelled at learning languages, among them Greek and Latin. At ten he passed on into high school, where he continued to excel. That year, 1930, his father also took him on a pilgrimage to the monastery at Czestochowa to see the Black Madonna, a Byzantine icon that has been of great importance to Poles since a seventeenth-century battle in which an undermanned army pushed back Swedish invaders with, it is believed, the help of the Virgin Mary. Young Karol's religious devotions continued to increase.

Like the town he grew up in, Wojtyla was different from many Poles in his association with and respect for Jews, with whom he

Young Karol with his class, seated in the second row from the front, second from the right.

felt a lifelong affinity. The house in which he was born was owned by a Jew, and several of his early playmates were Jewish, among them Jerzy Kluger, who remembers spending cold winter evenings with Lolek and his father, as the lieutenant (as he was always called) occupied the boys with stories of his military career. Since he attended a public rather than a Catholic school, Wojtyla had more contact with Jews than many of his Catholic contemporaries, which helped him escape the narrowing bonds of prejudice that afflicted so many of them. He even sometimes played goalie on a school soccer team dominated by Jewish boys, who played against a Catholic school team. Proof of Wojtyla's openhearted attitude toward Jews in general came decades later in his proclamation as pope in 1993 of the establishment of the Vatican's diplomatic relations with Israel.

When he was twelve, three years after his mother's death, Karol suffered his second personal tragedy. His brother, Edmund, who had graduated from medical school in Kraków, died of scarlet fever contracted from a patient. The quiet life of the remaining Wojtyla family became even more tinged with grief, yet still buttressed by faith. The loss of his mother and brother could not help but cause Karol to reflect with some melancholy on the hardships life imposes. His strongly held belief that suffering is not merely necessary but also a blessing visited upon those who endure it may be the result of his own method of dealing with personal reversals. It is also surely a product of the melding of his Polishness with the most abnegating strains of Catholic thought. The sense of not just necessary but also welcomed suffering that permeated both Wojtyla's nation and religion could not help but affect how he handled personal tragedy as it formed his concept of the world. Throughout his life, Woytyla not only accepted but also welcomed with an energetic optimism whatever misfortunes he was required to shoulder, considering them part of the price to be paid for eventual and eternal salvation.

❦ ❦ ❦

". . . he knew he was being led toward something more important."

As Karol entered his teen years, his life became a lengthening chain of activities, commitments, and interests. The hectic schedule he maintained was certainly driven by his avid mind and wide-ranging interests, and helped to fill the void in his life. It also allowed him to concentrate on something other than the bleakness that surrounded him. Although material wealth was not how Karol measured his life, Poland between the world wars was not a country of plenty, certainly not for families of the Wojtylas' restricted means. A high-school photograph of Wojtyla shows a bulky young man of strong facial features, with abundant dark hair combed straight back, a straight if somewhat overprominent nose, and a sharply defined chin. His eyes already bestowed the habitual merry squint that would become one of his most beloved papal trademarks. He was lively and well liked by those around him, with both male and female friends, but speculation that he once had a serious romantic attachment to a girl cannot be confirmed. As a woman friend from a later period in his life said, years after Wojtyla became pope: "He had every opportunity to have that kind of relationship if he had wanted to. But he knew he was being led toward something more important."

At this point, Karol was more interested in literature. In addition to being first in his class at the Wadowice high school, he acted in local dramatic productions as a leading member of a group called the Theater Circle and tinkered privately on ambitious works of poetry that dwelled on the human condition, while he read deeply of such Polish writers as Cyprian Norwid. Norwid, one of that nation's greatest poets and philosophers of the nineteenth century, was a fervent Polish nationalist with a love of country based on respect for human life. He was one of a group of nineteenth-century Romantic authors who claimed a messianic role for Poland as a nation that suffers so the world may live and be saved, but strong support for tolerance as well as his fierce love of his motherland made him one of Wojtyla's earliest heroes. As pope, Wojtyla often mentioned Norwid's brave challenge to his countrymen to respect each other, even as he crafted a similar message of his own.

In high school, Karol also met his first mentor outside of his father: Mieczyslaw Kotlarczyk, a teacher at a nearby girls' high school and creator of a dramatic theory called the Living Word. The style of the Living Word was based on precise and clear diction, with the goal of perfect annunciation of everything contained in the text. Dramatic effect would be achieved by the strength of words delivered with purity as opposed to the imposition of the actor's personality onto the character. Whether or not the Living Word style works in dramaturgical terms is debatable, but even its name, reminiscent of the Gospel of John, makes it seem like perfect preparation for one who would someday speak for Christ on Earth. Kotlarczyk assembled the Theater Circle to put his theories into practice, and Karol tackled the most difficult possible roles, becoming one of the main figures in the group.

But religion's pull still remained strong. Since his mother's death, he had gone to church every morning, and his deeply religious nature was well known to his friends. He joined a society that honored the Blessed Virgin Mary, the start of a lifelong, unflagging devotion, but he was also known for expressing his deep faith mainly in private. By the time he and his classmates began to think about high-school graduation, many of his friends assumed he would enter the priesthood, but he rejected the idea. His interest in speech, inspired by Kotlarczyk, led him toward wanting to study philology (now usually referred to as linguistics).

It was already common knowledge in Wadowice that Karol Wojtyla was unusually talented. His preeminence as a student was rewarded when, in 1938, he was chosen to greet a most important visitor to the school: the archbishop of Kraków, Prince Adam Sapieha. Titled scion of an aristocratic family, Sapieha was held in far higher regard than any secular authority in the city. For many years he had served Pope Pius X, creating powerful connections for himself at the Vatican. Only a personal grudge between him and the man who became Pope Pius XI had kept him from rising further in the Church's hierarchy. Sapieha was seventy years old at the time, tall and thin with graying hair cut short, and with piercing dark eyes. With his long, slender fingers wrapped around the crozier of his office, and a pectoral cross catching the light with every movement he made, he cut an impressive figure wherever he went. The effect at a school full of teenagers must have been electric. But so was Wojtyla's performance. He greeted the archbishop in the respectful tones due him, and welcomed him to the school. For the young man who had lived all his life in Wadowice, and had heard of Sapieha only in the most reverent tones, this would be the most important speech in his life to that point. He carried it off with the aplomb that would one day be his trademark. So impressed was Sapieha with the poise and politeness of the greeting offered by the young man that the cardinal asked Wojtyla's teacher if he was planning on becoming a priest. The answer disappointed him. Wojtyla, he was told, was thinking of attending college and studying philology. What a pity, remarked the archbishop. He did not bring up the matter again. But he did not forget the name Karol Wojtyla, either.

After graduating in May 1938, Wojtyla completed a required stint in a military labor battalion, working on road construction. Once that obligation was discharged, he and his father vacated the flat on Church Street in which the young man had lived his entire life and moved to Kraków so they could be together as Karol attended Jagiellonian University for a degree in philology. There they moved into a basement flat at 10 Tyniecka Street, downstairs from two sisters of Karol's mother.

Jagiellonian University was founded in 1364 by King Kazimierz the Great during what is considered Poland's Golden Age. Copernicus attended the school, and many centuries later Lenin read copiously in the university's libraries. The jewel of Polish higher learning, it had a decidedly progressive reputation in the 1930s. Karol plunged enthusiastically into the university life surrounding it. He expanded his already wide circle of friends by joining a new drama group, the local Marian society, and a number of literary discussion circles, though his socializing stopped short of bars; despite all his activities he was considered by friends a loner at heart. He continued to compose poetry as well, and became a frequent visitor to the fourteenth-century Wawel Cathedral, seat of the bishop of Kraków.

It was to its cool, dark recesses, perched above the Vistula River, that young Wojtyla walked on the morning of September 1, 1939. The Nazis had already begun their invasion of Poland that morning, and an air attack was engulfing Kraków. But after his mother's death Karol had committed himself to attending Mass every day and, fully aware of the danger, he made his way from his flat to the cathedral. The cathedral was empty—everyone else was too scared, or too sensible, to come, save for Father Figlewicz, his parish priest from Wadowice who now lived in Kraków. While Nazi planes strafed the city, Figlewicz said Mass as Wojtyla assisted. Karol knew that the world of his youth was over. It was the beginning of the Nazis' conquest of Poland and a foretaste of the war that would dominate Europe and much of the rest of the world for six years to come. Typically, Karol thought little of his own safety. Once Mass was over, he rushed to the home of some friends to make sure that they were uninjured.

Wojtyla and his father considered returning to Wadowice, where they thought they would be safer, but the father's deteriorating health made travel impossible. At age nineteen, Karol Wojtyla's once promising world had been converted virtually overnight into a life-and-death struggle for survival. And there was much worse to come.

Athens, 1946

CHAPTER TWO

ÜBER ALLES

◆

No country survives a war without changing. Few have been brutalized as mercilessly as Poland during World War II. The young and innocent Karol Wojtyla who reacted to the first Nazi pounding of Kraków by walking nonchalantly across a bridge to go to Mass did not just outlive the fighting. Instead, he was transformed into a committed, compassionate survivor who parried the cruelty of his homeland's enemies with intelligence, wit, and, above all, faith. If the future pope's unshakeable devotion and courage were instilled in him during his early childhood, his skills as a patriot and soldier for his God were honed during the war.

With the fall of Kraków and the subsequent invasion of eastern Poland by Soviet troops as a result of the Von Ribbentrop–Molotov pact, Poland once again became a war ground for its more powerful neighbors. The effect on Kraków was dramatic and painful. As much as the Nazis wanted to exterminate Poland and the Poles physically, they also wanted to destroy Poland's culture and religion. Wawel Cathedral was closed to the faithful, as was the city's theological seminary, which was supervised by Sapieha. Jagiellonian University was shuttered until further notice, and many of its professors were rounded up and deported to the Sachsenhausen concentration camp in Germany. Priests, nuns, and other members of religious orders were also arrested and sent to camps.

As terror crept through Kraków, along with the rest of Poland, residents realized that the world they knew was being dismantled and might, to future generations, just as well never have existed. A curfew was imposed. Writers, artists, and doctors were sent to camps. Random detention and execution or deportation to a death camp became daily possibilities. Shots echoing off the old walls of Kraków cut through the night.

Although to all appearances Karol Wojtyla's young life lay in ruins, he refused to be denied the things he considered most important. Though the university Karol attended had been closed by the Nazis, he continued his studies via a clandestine network of classes arranged by professors in hiding. The activities in which he found the greatest joy—worshiping God, reading and discussing poetry, performing in dramas— had become risky undertakings because of the Nazi attempt to destroy Polish culture, but he took part in secret literary discussion groups and acted in performances restricted to safe homes and tight circles of friends. He also turned out a prodigious flow of poems, as well as dramatic adaptations on biblical themes such as Job, David, and Jeremiah, and letters to the surprising number of friends with whom he kept in contact. But he could no longer count on his father's meager pension to keep them fed: The conquering Nazis had discontinued all benefits to Polish Army veterans. Thus, for the first time, the son became the source of support for the father. A lifetime of taking responsibility for others had begun. Karol worked at one of the few theaters that remained open, but even that job was soon gone, and the Wojtylas sank into poverty.

If he felt the weight of war pressing on him, Karol did not betray it publicly. Apart from his father, his main sources of inspiration was his friends. One of those new acquaintances was Jan Tyranowski, a Catholic zealot and self-styled philosopher who became one of the seminal influences on Wojtyla's life. Tyranowski was not, by the usual standards, an imposing figure. Thin, with a reedy voice, wispy mustache, and closely set eyes, Tyranowski was unmarried and employed as a tailor, a job that allowed him to work in silence and so devote most of his day to meditation. Like the clothes he fashioned for others, his worldly occupation was little more than a covering for the mystical Christian that he saw himself. He evinced little interest in the war, concentrating instead on preserving the spiritual purity that he believed—and that he taught Wojtyla—exists in each person. Unlike Karol, he was not universally liked. Tyranowski had a tendency to ask a lot of personal questions— possibly a sign of a winning lack of guile during peacetime, but during the Nazi occupation it often made people distrust him. Others found his religiosity too aggressive. He first encountered Wojtyla at a weekend prayer group, which, though not strictly prohibited by the Nazis, would certainly not have been sanctioned. Though he had achieved little material comfort or wordly success, Tyranowski was uncompromising in the area that drove his life—the human quest for salvation. It was Tyranowski, more than anyone, who was responsible for guiding Wojtyla to a religious vocation. It was Tyranowksi, then in his forties, who assumed the role of Wojtyla's spiritual mentor.

Tyranowski has been described by one of the pope's oldest friends, Father Mieczyslaw Malinski, who is still a priest in Kraków. Malinski met the future pontiff for the first time in 1940 at a rosary group organized by Tyranowski. After praying the beads, Tyranowski would encourage the young people in attendance to debate topics of religious interest, risky issues during the terrifying period of Nazi occupation. But meetings and group discussions were not enough for Tyranowski, nor did he permit his acolytes to spend idle time that he believed should be devoted to perfecting their religious practice. Each week, Malinski recalls, those who wished to remain in the group were summoned to meet with Tyranowski and describe their activities in detail in order to intensify their devotion, to bring them, literally, nearer to God. While Malinski found him "bossy" and old-fashioned, Karol felt otherwise.

In Karol Wojtyla, Tyranowski found an avid listener and disciple. Though calm on the outside, the young man was struggling to cope with what had happened to his country, his hopes, and his life; and the rigid spiritual discipline that Tyranowski managed to both preach and practice helped Karol maintain his control. By the summer of 1940, a lodger at a friend's house who was teaching Karol French had secured him a job at the Solvay chemical plant, which produced materials for explosives as well as water filtration. The job was breaking rocks at a quarry at Zakrzowek. Difficult as it was, it was a gilt-edged gift in war-ravaged Poland, since it provided Wojtyla with a prized internal document protecting him from arbitrary roundup and deportation to a death camp. Wojtyla was one of several young men of intellectual bent fortunate enough to be sent to Solvay, reportedly kept there by a bribe to the Gestapo.

Strapping and strong, Wojtyla made the most of the expe-

Wojtyla during World War II, at the Solvay Chemical plant.

rience, during which he acquired a lifelong affinity with those who earn their living with their hands. He made no complaint about the twelve-hour days during which he helped, first, to blast limestone from a quarry, and later to lay railroad tracks over which the limestone would be transported. Seeing that Wojtyla was not a common laborer, his fellow workers sometimes made accommodations for him, allowing him to rest or study while they slogged on. By no means, though, was his labor simple. One evening he collapsed from fatigue and was hit by a passing German truck. He lay unconscious overnight and was hospitalized for a time. It took him an hour to walk each way to work. Through this period, Tyranowski was at his side with prodding personal questions and a jabbing style of philosophical debate that helped develop Wojtyla's mind and spirit.

❧ ❧ ❧

". . . passing through the dark night of faith . . ."

Wojtyla had shown courage and strength in the face of every hardship up to that point, but he was not prepared for the next shock in his life. Not long after Christmas 1940, Karol's father became ill and could no longer take care of himself or their home. Already exhausted physically by his work at Solvay, Karol now had to fetch dinner, prepared by friends, for his father and do his best to keep house. On February 18, 1941, twenty-year-old Karol walked into his apartment with a tin pot of food in each hand and found that his father had died, alone.

Remorse at not being at his father's side as he slid toward death battled with overwhelming personal sadness. One by one every member of his family had died, and Karol Wojtyla was now completely alone. For the first time, Wojtyla's friends feared that he had encountered a tragedy from which he would not rebound. But it was Tyranowski—pugnacious, uncompromising, and single-minded—who filled the vacuum and became the force that shaped Karol Wojtyla's destiny. Tyranowski affected Wojtyla in many ways, but none was more profound or lasting than his introduction of the young man to the mysticism of St. John of the Cross.

Juan de Yepes y Alvarez, born in 1542 in Fontiveros, Spain, had become a Carmelite monk, embracing that twelfth-century order's devotion to poverty, abstinence, and contemplation. The movement, originally founded with the intention of continuing the hermetic lifestyle of the Old Testament prophet Elijah, had lost much of its fervor by the time John joined it. He met and combined forces with a Carmelite nun who would one day become St. Teresa of Avila, to establish a reform wing of the order in 1569. They became known as the Discalced, or Barefoot, Carmelites, rejecting the moderating influences of the Calced Carmelites and demonstrating their devotion to complete poverty by wearing sandals instead of shoes.

John's willingness to suffer was integral to his bedrock belief that adversity of any kind not only contributed to but also was essential to salvation. His densely worded poetry, including *Spiritual Canticle* and *The Dark Night of the Soul*, glorifies the opportunities that suffering brings. "The soul sings of the fortunate adventure that it had in passing through the dark night of faith, to union with the beloved," he wrote. Though it is difficult today to imagine two Catholic orders engaged in actual combat, the Calced and Discalced wings of the Carmelites were mortal foes. John's finest poetry was written behind bars, where he spent years in custody of the Calceds.

Even while he grieved for his father, Wojtyla allowed himself to see the joy that could await him—the kind of joy described by St. John of the Cross—if he followed Tyranowski's plan for his future and committed himself to a life in the service of God. It was the central decision of his life, and one that was shaped in equal parts by sorrow and mysticism. In the midst of war, loneliness, and personal despair, he set himself on the course that would lead him one day to don the Shoes of the Fisherman.

❧ ❦ ❧

"When we heard that he was going to become a priest, we all despaired."

That decision, still in its embryonic stages, did not mean that young Karol had forsaken other pleasures, such as they were in wartime Kraków. In 1941 his friend Mieczyslaw Kotlarczyk moved to Kraków, and along with other friends interested in drama, they created the underground Rhapsodic Theater, a drama group that put on clandestine performances of patriotic Polish plays for select audiences. Given its nationalist orientation, it was a dangerous undertaking, and soon ties were made with Unia, an arm of the military resistance concerned with cultural issues.

It was in the Rhapsodic Theater that he met, among others, Danuta Michalowska, an aspiring actress with whom he shared several theatrical credits. She recalls him as a natural thespian. "He was renowed, truly excellent," she said years later. "Had he decided to stay an actor, he'd have been a great one. I've told him that several times when I've seen him since he's become pope, and he always just smiles and shakes his head. He had a beautiful voice, artistic expression, good imagination that allowed him to depict various shades of the roles that he played. We rehearsed so many roles together that I can say it with assurance: He was the best. When we heard that he was going to become a priest, we all despaired."

It was not just fellow actors who wondered at his decision about a vocation. His friend from the theater Kotlarczyk also tried to talk him out of becoming a priest. Another friend, Tadeusz Kudlinski, who was closely associated with the Rhapsodic Theater, spent several hours trying to dissuade Wojtyla from the priesthood, says Michalowska. At first, Wojtyla told his acquaintances that he wished to become a Carmelite monk. Although Kudlinski was finally able to convince him to become a dioscesan priest, using the argument that in that way he could at least continue his writing; in the end, Wojtyla had listened not to the friends he valued so much but to the voice within him that was calling him to an even greater challenge.

❖ ❖ ❖

"... a dangerous choice."

Archbishop Sapieha was told of Wojtyla's desire. Sapieha had little regard for the enemy who occupied his homeland. By 1942, he had become a leading figure in the opposition to Nazi rule, actively aiding Jews and trying to notify the Vatican of the Nazi genocide. He was also involved in underground activities, which included the creation of a secret seminary that Karol entered in October 1942 as one of the first ten

RHAPSODIC THEATER

Resistance to foreign powers can take place under various guises. Some employ their courage by facing bullets and imprisonment. Others resist by keeping their conquered country's culture alive. On August 22, 1941, with Poland under Nazi rule, Wojtyla along with his friends Mieczyslaw Kotlarczyk and Tadeusz Kudlinski, founded an underground drama group they called the Rhapsodic Theater. Wojtyla's natural stage presence and careful elocution made him the outstanding male in the group. He worked with three actresses: Krystyna Debowska, Halina Krolikiewicz, and Danuta Michalowska. In an interview in her Kraków flat in 1994, Michalowska still displayed the broad gestures, pauses for effect, and dramatic timing that made her such a standout a half century earlier. Her recollections of her colleague were etched as clearly in her mind as a well-studied script.

"I met Karol for the first time in 1940, soon after he'd arrived from Wadowice. At the time he was in university and I was in secondary school. Karol was never outspoken about resistance to the Germans, but this was because it was not nec-essary for him to say anything. It was obvious how he felt and equally obvious that he was willing to do whatever he believed was required of him to end the occupation of our beloved country."

What he chose to do might be described as indirect resistance, yet in the young Wojtyla's mind, it was crucial. He unhesitatingly took an oath to the underground organization known as Unia which existed under the patronage of Archbishop Sapieha. Rather than staging military sabotage against the Germans, Unia devoted itself to preserving Poland's cultural identity.

As Michalowska, still proudly recalling those years of stuggle, put it: "What we did didn't involve guns or bombs. It involved words. We created works of art that I believe were important to our country's survival through those dreadful times. And Wojtyla was the guiding light of the group both artistically and through his personality. He's told me many times that his technique of speaking, of making each person who hears him think that the pope is speaking directly to him, was learned while he was a member of the Rhapsodic Theater."

To understand the pressure under which he lived, it helps to recall that Wojtyla was carrying three full-time occupations under war conditions. He was employed in the Solvay quarry, work that was exhausting and that forced him to spend hours commuting from his home. He was studying to become a priest, which was prohibited by the Nazis. But that did not mean that Sapieha, never one to bend his view of the world, would relax the requirements imposed on any man who wished to serve God in the diocese of Kraków. Finally, Wojtyla was taking part in the Rhapsodic Theater's rehearsals and performances, the quality of which were outstandingly high, considering the war conditions.

Because Wojtyla, even as a young man, insisted on giving his utmost to each commitment he made, the Unia underground leadership released him from his membership oath so he could concentrate on his seminary studies. His final performance with the Rhapsodic Theater was in March 1943. The theater itself continued in existence after the Nazis had been driven from Poland, but its postwar mission was essentially the same. Because the Soviet-dominated Communist government viewed Polish patriotic drama and literature with suspicion, the Rhapsodic Theater remained a banned organiza-

tion. In 1958 Wojtyla wrote an article in the Catholic weekly *Tygodnik Powszechny* arguing that the Rhapsodic Theater should be legalized. "This theater, in which there is so much word and relatively little acting, safeguards young actors against developing a destructive individualism, because it will not let them impose on the text anything of their own. It gives them inner discipline."

These were the same arguments Wojtyla, as John Paul II, would make in later years to justify the strict regime by which he expected members of the Church to live.

The theater, which was briefly legalized, was closed down for good by the Communist authorities in 1967. For Danuta Michalowska, however, it will always remain a vibrant memory of her past, and her kindred association with the young man who helped found and nurture it. Today, she says of her friend Karol Wojtyla: "He's a man living alone, that's obvious. He had to give up any ideas about that kind of life long ago. But the fullness with which he lived his life, back when we were working in the Rhapsodic Theater and even after he became pope, has been an example to all people that God has a plan for us. He is fulfilling that plan, and he provides us all with an example of how to live life."

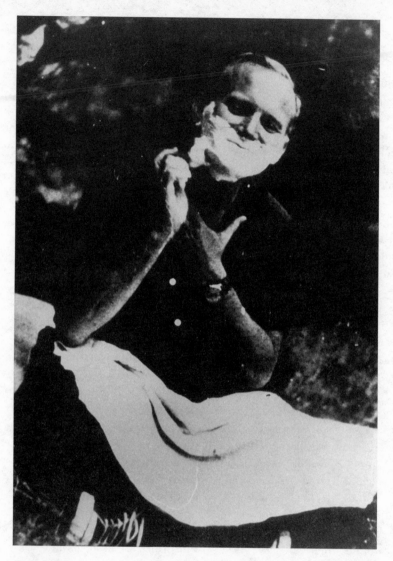

Wojtyla always enjoyed the outdoors, here in the Polish mountains.

seminarians. Karol's decision cut him off not only from many of the other endeavors in which he showed such talent; it was also a dangerous choice. He continued to work at the plant and put on plays with the Rhapsodic Theater, but he was released from his oath of membership in Unia. Seminary instruction was secret and on a one-to-one basis, not only to escape detection but also to avoid any one person knowing more than they absolutely had to, since the Nazi punishment for becoming a seminarian was execution or deportation to a death camp.

By 1944, however, the Nazis were growing more desperate. The Warsaw uprising of August 1, 1944, drove the Nazis to round up all men between fifteen and fifty on August 6 to transport them to work details or labor camps. From house to house the Nazis swept through Kraków, arresting every man of those ages they could find. When news of the crackdown came to Karol, he fell to his knees in his room and prayed. The Nazis came to his home, but for whatever reason did not search the basement where he was staying. Karol remained a free man, but Sapieha decided it was time to bring him in. He instructed all the seminarians to move immediately into hiding in his residence so they could safely complete their studies.

By abandoning his job at the chemical plant to pursue the priesthood, Wojtyla put himself in direct danger from the Nazis. But after more than five years of German occupation, Poles had begun to feel a sense of optimism that the Allies would eventually win the war. Wojtyla, living in hiding in the archbishop's palace, never stepped onto the streets of the city he had come to consider his own until the war ended. The Nazis began to look for Wojtyla, who had simply disappeared from his job at Solvay, until the manager of the plant was convinced by Sapieha through an intermediary to illegally take his name off the rolls.

"... the presence of the Holy Spirit was very strong from the beginning."

It was a confining life, but for the young men whom Sapieha had taken into his residence, seclusion was part of the inner peace they were seeking. The living conditions were cramped and bleak. For Wojtyla it also meant a break with Tyranowski, his mentor and the man who, after his father, had been the most important influence on his inner life. Though Tyranowski was able to occasionally visit the seminary, Wojtyla was now under the aegis of Sapieha.

By January 1945 the Germans had finally left Kraków, and Wojtyla was able to pursue his studies with the breakneck enthusiasm with which he did most things. Mieczyslaw Malinski, who followed Wojtyla into the seminary, remembers that his friend talked about himself as though he were already ordained. "For him, the presence of the Holy Spirit was very strong from the beginning," Malinski recalls, and Wojtyla did not understand that other candidates for the priesthood might still be wrestling with doubts.

While Poland tried to come to terms with the destruction it had suffered during the war, Wojtyla concentrated his extraordinary mind on the goal of the priesthood. By late 1946 he had completed an essay on the mysticism of St. John of the Cross. And on November 1, 1946—the solemn holy day of All Saints—Karol Wojtyla became a priest of the Roman Catholic

Church, ordained by Sapieha. He celebrated first Mass of his priesthood in the crypt of St. Leonard in Wawel Castle, among the tombs of Polish kings. At age twenty-six, he had found his mission in life.

circa 1956

CHAPTER THREE

Uncle Wojtyla

———◆———

If Karol's twenty-six years as a layman were defined by the spiritual and intellectual focuses to which he had devoted himself, his early life as a priest was a whirlwind of the prodigious energy for which he had finally found a worthy outlet. Two weeks after his ordination, he was—on Sapieha's orders—aboard a train bound for Rome, the city over which he would one day preside as bishop. This was no tourist excursion. Wojtyla was being sent from the Kraków diocese to the theological college in Rome administered by the Dominicans, the Angelicum, to earn an advanced degree in theology. For a year and a half Wojtyla had the luxury of doing what he loved best—learning and praying—while at the same time fulfilling the wishes of his patron. Rome in the immediate aftermath of war was a city of devastation and defeat. But for Wojtyla, after the ravaged landscape of Poland, it was both the cradle of faith and a miracle of sensory fulfillment. Although Wojtyla gave first priority to his studies, he still found time to explore the history and majesty of the Eternal City. The young priest who told friends in Poland of his trips to the catacombs and the great cathedrals also became familiar with the working class of the city, who spoke to him of their workaday concerns—the stuff that would continue to occupy and bedevil him as pope three decades later.

Wojtyla's learning curve rose sharply in Rome, on many different levels. His academic studies, the equivalent of a course leading to a master's degree, were intense, but he also found time to drink in the city's cultural wonders and to make acquaintances within the normally closed bureaucracy of the Vatican. Further, his excursions to small towns and villages throughout Italy, France, and Belgium put him in contact with the everyday Catholics the Church is committed to serve. It was while on those expeditions that Wojtyla learned firsthand about the post-war experiments in Catholicism that would affect his Church significantly later in the century. The concept of "worker-priests" living and laboring with the lay members of their parishes seemed to Wojtyla, who had himself done heavy manual chores during the war, to bridge the gap that divides clerics from their flocks and can make priests appear aloof and unconcerned with everyday concerns such as low wages and work-related fatigue.

No stranger himself to exhausting labor, Wojtyla became interested in the concept of the clergy taking a more direct role in laypeople's everyday lives. In the summer of 1947 he and another young Polish priest traveled to Marseilles to see firsthand the theological-sociological experiment being conducted by worker-priests such as Jacques Loew, who shouldered the same physical burdens as the dockworkers of that French city.

It was by establishing the link of trust built on common labor that Loew and other priests like him hoped to reverse the trend away from Church attendance in post-war France. Some worker-priests strayed from that original goal and became

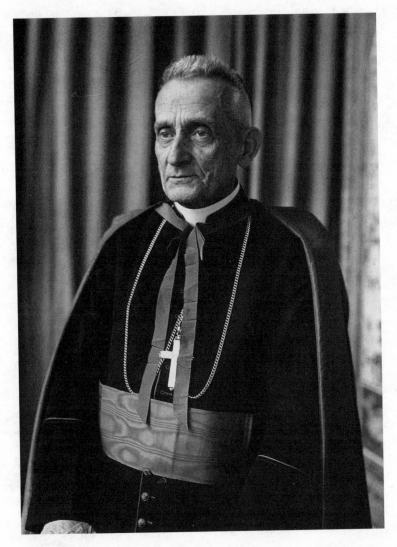

Archbishop Adam Sapieha of Kraków.

ST. THOMAS AQUINAS

It is not surprising that John Paul II would feel a special affinity with St. Thomas Aquinas, given certain similarities in their upbringings and in their natures. Aquinas was born in 1225, the son of a landowner in northern Italy. When he was five he was placed in a Benedictine monastery to be raised and educated, and at 14 he began to attend the University of Naples, where he encountered the writings of Aristotle, which were then to filtering back into Western thought.

Here he also encountered the Dominicans, a mendicant order not unlike the Discalced Carmelites that Wojtyla considered joining at the same age. Despite opposition from his family, who actually had him imprisoned to prevent him from becoming a Dominican, Aquinas joined the order of his choice and quickly earned renown. Aquinas's most famous work, the *Summa Theologiae*, is a long, intricate tapestry of logical arguments in defense of Christianity and the beliefs of the Catholic Church. The profundity of its thought and the breadth of its relevence has left the scholars of the last seven hundred years debating whether he is best called a philosopher or a theologian.

St. Thomas Aquinas and his cerebral approach to God and Man appealed to Wojtyla, who approached the world with a similar academic rigor. The logic of Aquinas's arguments gave an intellectual underpinning to Wojtyla's faith, as it had to so many Catholics before him, and possibly Aquinas himself became of role model of sorts for young Karol, not just in the quality of his thought, but in their quantity as well: According to Timothy McDermott, Aquinas left approximately eight and a half million words, enough to dwarf John Paul II's prodigious output.

The deep influence of Aquinas's thought shows in Wojtyla's sense of man's natural obligation to perform good and in his support of a Third Way for human society between capitalism and communism. To Aquinas, the state's "goal and justification is to offer to man satisfactory material conditions of life as a basis for a moral and intellectual education which, in turn, must be such as to lend itself to the spiritual edification of the Christian man." Though both Aquinas and Wojtyla recognize the necessity of collaborative activity among people and the validity of economics, to them the goal is, as in all things, the greater glory of God.

enmeshed in secular politics, usually on the side of leftist causes. That deviation never tempted Wojtyla, whose native land was about to slip behind the dark post-war shadow of the Iron Curtain.

Inevitably, the leftward drift of the movement attracted the opposition of traditionalists within the hierarchy of the Church. Pope Pius XII recognized the merits of reaching out to workers as a way of keeping them within the fold, but worried that any alliance with the growing socialist movements in Europe would be misinterpreted as sympathy for the aggressively expanding Soviet Union. As a result, the worker-priest experiment was condemned by several influential theologians and its full potential was never reached.

The young Polish priest spent his summer in various worker-priest communities. He wrote about what he encountered, even publishing an article in the Polish Catholic weekly *Tygodnik Powszechny*, where he would become a regular contributor. No doubt his experiences contributed to the vision he maintained throughout his papacy of a third path between communism and unfettered capitalism, both of which he believed harmful to man's spiritual well-being.

The more intellectual pull of St. Thomas Aquinas also acted as a balance to the influence of the worker-priest experiment on Karol. Most appealing to him was Thomas's insistence that in the event of a conflict between reason and faith, Catholics are duty-bound to adhere to the Church's teaching. Thus, even though scientific evidence and modern learning point us in one direction, Thomism commands the faithful to act in a way mandated by God and interpreted by the Church, even if that means rejecting commonly accepted knowledge. Thomas would be unmoved by arguments that the Church is behind the times. The times, he would respond, were created by God, not man, and so are subject to His laws, not their own.

After completing a second year of training at the Angelicum, Wojtyla returned to Kraków brimming with ideas about the holy life he was undertaking. Sapieha, always one step ahead, surprised the young priest by dispatching him to an out-of-the-way rural parish east of Kraków. The village, Niegowici, was in a Polish backwater that had survived Nazi occupation better than the country's cities. That did not mean, however, that it was a country paradise. The conditions were so rough that many assumed Sapieha was punishing Wojtyla, who had previously appeared to be one of his favorites; what they did not know was that many priests of whom much was expected were sent to Niegowici as a test of sorts.

❧ ❧ ❧

"Be not afraid!"

Wojtyla passed the test. While serving there, he lived humbly in a wooden house that let in the winter's bitter cold. Nevertheless, he took pains to adapt to the less sophisticated traditions of bucolic life. He walked everywhere, endured the cold of winter without complaint, and found a way to enjoy the beauty of nature without grousing about the village's cultural shortcomings. If he was disappointed to be kept away from his adopted home any longer than necessary, Wojtyla never let on. Indeed, almost from the day of his arrival, he encouraged the parishioners to form a drama club, a rosary society, a stronger parish committee. The young priest immediately zeroed in on the parish's young people, organizing and participating in soccer matches, country walks, hymn-singing. At each new event in which he took part, he gave evidence of his unshakable faith in God. His greatest triumph presaged some of his later showdowns with the Communists then taking over Poland: the construction of a new church. Though the authorities did not want it built, Wojtyla instigated the fund drive, and used volunteer labor. The church was finally consecrated in 1958.

After less than a year in Niegowici, Sapieha recalled his young rising star in 1949 to the city they both loved, and installed him in St. Florian's, a twin-steepled brick church in Kraków and one of the most upscale of the city's parishes. Sapieha knew that he would need all the talent he could muster. Poland was about to enter another era of occupation, this time by Communists.

The rise of communism in Poland was by and large peaceful and legitimate. Still recovering from the horrors inflicted on Poland by the Germans, voters in 1948 gave the Polish United Workers' Party a victory in national elections. At about the same time, the newly assertive Soviet Union, reveling in its status as one of the war's victorious Allies, annexed the Ukraine and parts of eastern Poland, and was met with virtual silence in the West. The Communists in Warsaw then followed Moscow's lead and initiated a policy to curb the extensive influence of the Catholic Church. But unlike other countries pulled into the Soviet Union's orbit, Poland remained a bedrock of faith, with nearly 99 percent of the population baptized into the Church. The regime had identified its enemy but also knew it would have to move cautiously.

Further complicating the Communists' strategy, the Polish Church had selected Bishop Stefan Wyszynski of Lublin, a canon lawyer, as the country's primate, the de facto leader of its Catholic Church. Wyszynski was instinctively and viscerally anti-Communist, but was also wise enough to know that the Church could not win an outright contest of attrition against the newly powerful government apparatus. Unlike the regal Sapieha, who found it difficult to give ground on any matter, Wyszynski was experimenting with and developing the subtle art of coexistence with the Communists, as one part of an overall strategy of resistance and survival.

After watching Communist regimes imprison clerics and attempt to crush the Church throughout Eastern Europe, Wyszynski expressed his willingness in 1949 to make a deal. Knowing the depth of Catholic belief in their nation, the Communist authorities realized that some accommodations would be necessary if the people were to confer any degree of legitimacy on their government. Both sides sat down, and lengthy negotiations finally resulted in a document in 1950 that made the pope the highest Church authority on issues of "faith, morality, and Church jurisdiction." Otherwise, the Polish Church would be directed by the national interests of Poland. Though some saw this as a surrender, the agreement allowed the Catholic Church to continue functioning and, as history would bear out, play a decisive role in the eventual dissolution of Communist rule in Poland.

For Father Wojtyla, St. Florian's could hardly have been less like his first parish assignment, nor could it have matched the young priest's personal interests more closely. St. Florian's was a traditional haunt of Kraków's large student community. Located near the city's Old Town, it also attracted its share of intellectuals, many of whom voiced their ideas and discontent with the stultifying onset of Communist dictatorship. Wojtyla plunged into the new duties with vigor. As much as he had enjoyed the outdoor existence of his first assignment, he was equally at home in the refined atmosphere of a progressive city parish. Just as he had made use of the glory of nature while he was in the country, now he organized field expeditions for the youth of St. Florian. His preferred activities were overnight camping in the Tatra Mountains and kayaking trips along the rivers that course through southern Poland. But even that was not enough for him. His friend Father Malinski notes that while he dazzled parishioners with his grasp of philosophical and theological questions, the young Wojtyla was quietly turning out an enormous quantity of poetry, drama, and essays. Some were published under pseudonyms, but most he kept under wraps until later. Among the works that Wojtyla probably began during his early priesthood were the lengthy poem *Song of Reflecting Water* and a play titled *Our God's Brother*, based on the life of a nineteenth-century Kraków painter who founded an order of religious brothers. While the writing in both works is densely packed with thought and devotion, their main message is more down to earth: Be not afraid! Allow the just anger born of Christ in your hearts to give you strength. If you keep that anger alive, the forces will come to channel it into change.

Still, his intellectual potential was not being fully realized. With the death of Jan Tyranowski, who contracted a fatal infection and died in agony in 1947, Wojtyla had only his aging cardinal to guide him. Sapieha, declining in health but still comfortably in control of Poland's Catholic Church organization, received regular reports on the progress of his most promising young priests. Sensing his own end was near, he gave instructions as to how his acolytes should be handled after he was gone. To Wojtyla's enormous grief, Sapieha died in 1951, but the aging prelate had first instructed his successor as to how he wanted Wojtyla's career to progress. Thus the young priest-scholar was ordered to take a leave from his parish and undertake a second doctoral thesis. His first, completed in Rome, had examined the mysticism of St. John of the Cross. The second attempted to define the ethics

St. Florian's in Kraków, Wojtyla's second parish assignment.

of Christianity using the work of Max Scheler, a half-Jewish German phenomenologist. Scheler's philosophical writings sought to establish the relationship between the development of attitudes and human actions. In brief, Scheler wanted to know what makes us do the things we do, a question that consumed Wojtyla throughout his life.

If his latest assignment kept him more out of the public eye than he might have wished, it was just as well. During the final days of Stalin's murderous reign in Moscow, the Polish Communist regime was intensifying its persecution of priests. Even Wyszynski felt its sting. When he was consecrated a cardinal in November 1952, the authorities refused to let him travel to Rome to receive the red hat that signified his elevation as a prince of the Church. But though Wojtyla was not yet noticed by the Communists, his never-ending supply of energy and ideas were becoming a minor legend among the faithful of Kraków. Even as he labored on his thesis, he found time to lead camping, skiing, and kayaking trips for the young people who seemed drawn to him as today's youths are attracted to rock stars. When he began wearing black horn-rimmed glasses for the myopia that blurred his vision, his young admirers tagged him with the label "Uncle," as much a sign of affection as one that could disguise him in case Communist authorities came upon these unsanctioned Church activities.

The young people's admiration was not based on Wojtyla's liberal attitudes or any suggestion from him that "anything goes." At a moment when their country was under assault from an ideology that subjugated both Polish national pride and historic Catholic loyalty to a series of Five-Year Plans for production, the smiling priest who had spent a year in Rome and exuded quiet confidence was a reassuring presence. Using the same actor's skills with which he managed to fool his Nazi employers in the quarry during the war as he studied for the priesthood under their eyes, Wojtyla communicated a sly sense of rebellion to his youthful charges. Do not be intimidated by these Communists, he was telling them with his twinkling eyes and square-set jaw. They count for little next to the love of Jesus. In his leadership style as well as in his writings, the message was: Be not afraid, stay righteously angry.

Although he was opposed to the atheism implicit in Soviet-style communism, Wojtyla was not a supporter of capitalism, either. His travels through Western Europe had shown him that the excesses of market economies were also harmful to the well-being of the soul. Wojtyla had not yet publicly expressed his thoughts on the matter, but they were fermenting inside his capacious mind, waiting for the moment when he could offer a third way to the world.

❖ ❖ ❖

"I have two responsibilities to youth: canoeing and skiing."

His reputation spread among Catholic intellectuals, and by the mid-1950s "Uncle" Wojtyla, who insisted he would just as soon be strumming his guitar in front of a campfire, was in great demand as a speaker at Church-sponsored gatherings throughout Poland. Father Andrzej Bardecki, who wrote for the Kraków Catholic newspaper *Tygodnik Powszechny*, recalls Wojtyla telling him: "I have two responsibilities to youth: canoeing and skiing."

Among the signal honors he received was an invitation to lecture at the Catholic University of Lublin, the only Catholic institution of higher learning behind the Iron Curtain. Father Malinski, who stayed in close touch with his friend from the clandestine seminary, believes that these years of intensive writing, lecturing, prayer, and physical recreation were the happiest in Wojtyla's life.

Wojtyla with Stefan Cardinal Wyszynski, far left.

That happy and productive interlude came to a shattering end in 1956, when Polish security forces opened fire on striking workers in Poznan, killing and wounding hundreds. The massacre at Poznan resolved any ambiguity most Poles had about the willingness of their Communist leaders to shed Polish blood for ideological reasons. Some had argued that the Communists were preferable to the Nazis, but the 1956 incident—along with the Soviets' crushing of the Hungarian uprising—shattered any illusions that socialism was a form of freedom. Having ministered to workers as well as intellectuals, Wojtyla had the doubly difficult task of helping them come to terms with a tragedy that he had foreseen as inevitable. The détente with the regime by Stefan Wyszynski (he had been made a cardinal in 1953) might have been discredited had the Communist authorities followed through with the military crackdown that Soviet leader Nikita Khrushchev was demanding. Instead, the government came to terms with the strikers, who wanted a decent wage increase to offset the price hikes that had been imposed. As further evidence of its goodwill, the government resolved to stop harassing Church leaders as openly as it had in the past. It was a solid vindication of Wyszynski's policy and a lesson that was not lost on Father Wojtyla.

Inevitably, Wojtyla's exceptional mind and outstanding pastoral qualities brought him to the attention of the Church hierarchy. Still in his mid-thirties, he became chairman of the ethics department at the university in Lublin, and delivered a series of lectures that stand as early milestones in his complicated, lifelong struggle to come to terms with God's loving plans for man and the human responsibility to accept those divine wishes. Although it was not yet published, the young priest-philosopher was also working on a book that would demonstrate the scope of his compassion for his fellow human beings, and his determination to help them live their lives according to God's will. He titled it *Love and Responsibility*.

But nothing—not lectures, riots, or the frantic commuting he did between Lublin and Kraków—was permitted to short-change him of the outdoor adventures he and his young followers savored. So it was that in August 1958, while kayaking with students, he learned that he had been nominated an auxiliary bishop of Kraków. Father Malinski delights in recounting the tale of how Wojtyla, who had no opportunity to clean himself up before going to see Cardinal Wyszynski, turned up in Warsaw and gratefully accepted the honor that had been bestowed on him. Then, with the winning, slightly mischievous grin that would one day become his trademark around the world, he asked if he was now permitted to return to the river where his friends were waiting for him. At age thirty-eight, Karol Wojtyla had been plucked from the ranks of ordinary priesthood to join the leadership of the Catholic Church.

circa 1967

CHAPTER FOUR

THE COUNCIL

———◆———

Who is this Wojtyla? wondered the Communist authorities in Warsaw. Of course, they knew through the machinery of their system exactly who Karol Wojtyla was, where he was born and educated. But what justified his being made a bishop?

In a short time, the answer would become all too clear. As a priest, lecturer, and chaplain, Wojtyla had been content to influence only those with whom he had daily contact: his young followers, the faculty and students at the Catholic university and at St. Florian's, the parishioners who came to him for advice and comfort. Almost immediately upon becoming a bishop, however, he found his voice in national affairs.

Until then he had focused his attention on youth, on intellectuals, on workers, speaking with them on their level. Through those seemingly pedestrian contacts, the weekly prayer meetings, the regular shifts as confessor and confidant, he had heard firsthand of the problems that postwar Polish Catholics were encountering. And through those contacts he had also formed opinions that would remain with him throughout his life.

Though the Communists sometimes tried to play Wojtyla and Wyszynski off each other—the former as young and forward-looking, the latter as prewar and conservative—Wojtyla had learned too much to fall for such a strategy. He held to Wyszynski's basic precepts for handling the Communists: Be as tough as they are; don't back them into a corner; and make a fuss for the things that rightly affect the Church.

One of his most persistent criticisms of the Communist regime was that those who believed in God were penalized, whereas those who either pretended to be, or genuinely were, atheists, were treated in a better fashion. This, the under-forty bishop argued, reduced Catholics to lying about fundamental faith and beliefs, thus making a mockery not only of the Church but also of all society. Be not afraid! he told his congregations. Your right to believe in God cannot be taken away from you. In making such strong pronouncements, Wojtyla was once again employing the tactic he had used successfully as a young priest: He made the seemingly all-powerful Communists less intimidating by making them, and not their opponents, appear to be the ones out of step with Polish reality. Let them occupy the government ministries and drive around in official cars, he seemed to be saying. You and I know that they are phonies, and that what we believe in—the love of God and His Son, Jesus Christ—is far more relevant to our daily lives.

Such sentiments were bound to attract the wrath of a government that knew it held on to power only because its neighbor, the Soviet Union, would permit no other party to rule. Father Malinski believes that Wojtyla, even at that early point in his life, knew that what he was doing would draw attention to himself and invite a danger to which he had not until then been exposed. He told Malinski once that no matter how difficult the Communists made it for them, he felt certain that the Church would prevail. Though no political expert or historian was then saying it, Karol Wojtyla had an instinct that told him communism could not survive.

There was another force gathering, one that in Wojtyla's estimation carried far greater power and importance. Nearly as soon as he was elected in late 1958, the new pope, John XXIII, announced that he would summon the bishops and cardinals of the Catholic Church to Rome to take part in an ecumenical (universal) council at the Vatican. Although this would be the twenty-first ecumenical council in the Church's 2,000-year history, it would be only the second at the Vatican, the seat of the papacy, bearing witness to the council's importance and potential for creating change. In essence, it was a call to the leaders of Roman Catholicism to debate and discuss all aspects of the Church; a chance to redefine its stand on questions about the basics of their faith. It was the equivalent of a country writing a new constitution that would redefine its citizens' rights, expectations, and responsibilities. It was also a one-time opportunity to position the Church for the end of the second millennium and prepare it for the third.

Pope John sensed that the Church he had been elected to lead needed a spirit of renewal, or as the participants themselves put it, "to adapt more closely to the needs of our age those institutions that are subject to change; to foster whatever can promote union among all those who believe in Christ; to strengthen whatever can help to call all mankind into the Church's fold." Of course, doing so ran the risk of alienating those within the Church who wanted no change, who thought that the traditions that had sustained the Church since Christ's death were worthy of preservation for the very reason that they had proven their durability.

The Catholic Church is in the business of saving souls, but for the men who serve it as senior members of the clergy, it is also a lifelong profession, and like any working place, it has its internal politics. Thus for the 108 cardinals and more than 2,500 archbishops and bishops who were invited to St. Peter's Basilica, the Council was both a golden opportunity and a minefield. Nearly three years elapsed between John XXIII's announcement and its actual convening, and in that time there had been endless discussion, both written and less formal, among Church elders about the agenda. The 2,300 bishops and other prelates who took part in Vatican II were required to do a massive amount of preparation. An agenda of more than 2,000 pages was sent to each participant, who was expected to read it and master the details of each topic for discussion. The bishops and cardinals were assisted in their work by a large number of *periti*—clerical experts on subjects of Church dogma and degrees, who prepared reams of preparatory reports, position papers, and options for the men who would shape the course of the Church. Like the preparatory reports, these documents were also meant to be read and used.

John XXIII opened the first session of the Council on October 11, 1962. His welcoming speech was stilted by any modern standard of media event, but John was not a pope concerned with the quality of his sound bytes. Nor would he see the Council's work through to its end. He died on June 3, 1963, and was succeeded by Giovanni Battista Cardinal Montini, who took the name Paul VI. Though Vatican II will always be remembered as John XXIII's initiative, it was under Paul that it completed its most important work.

Although Wojtyla was only an auxiliary bishop, his brother Poles knew that his was one of the finest minds their land had to offer. Like any young man with big ideas and a desire to be heard, Wojtyla tried to prepare himself for the biggest business meeting of his life by learning in advance what topics would be most important, which cardinals and bishops stood on which side of the issues, and what arguments they would offer. In gathering this intelligence, he relied on contacts and acquaintances he had made during his earlier stay in Rome as a student. He also sought out other bishops, with whom he began the delicate process of forming personal alliances. These relationships would one day be the key to his election as successor of St. Peter.

As always, Wojtyla's work habits were both odd and awe-inspiring. He rose early each day to say a private Mass, then spent some time writing and reflecting before walking to the Vatican from the Polish Institute, where he slept and pored over Council documents. Once in his place, Wojtyla astounded those around him by placidly preparing lectures that he planned to give back in Poland and, even more outlandishly, writing poetry while other speakers presented their addresses. Such conduct might have earned him a reputation for disrespect had it not been for the Polish bishop's uncanny ability at the end of each Council workday to summarize, accurately and with extraordinary incisiveness, the arguments that had been heard. Wojtyla's ability to write, pray, or reflect while listening to a discourse or even taking part in a separate conversation is only one of his unexplained abilities. Another is his apparent comfort in listening to visitors speak several different languages to him, and managing to respond to each in the same tongue, fluently, without getting them confused. It did not go unremarked by the other participants at the Council, many of them bishops who would later be called to Rome to elect him pope in 1978.

For his part, when he was given the opportunity to speak, he made the most of it. On November 7, 1962, he delivered an address, using the excellent Latin he had mastered at school in Wadowice, on the role of the sacraments in defining Church liturgy. He also penned two documents that would be considered part of the Council's overall work. While those may seem like minor contributions in a gathering as vast as the Vatican Council, they were well received, and marked the young bishop from Kraków as a comer. In later years his detractors would point out the apparent contradictions between his enthusiastic participation in Vatican II, which he never regretted, and the widespread impression that his papacy was devoted to undoing many of the liberalizing trends the Council set in motion.

❧ ❧ ❧

"... they were absolutely aghast that a priest would write a book like this."

Earlier in the year, Wojtyla published the book he had been working on for years, *Love and Responsibility*. For its time, and considering who its author was, the work was nothing short of revolutionary. It takes a relatively no-holds-barred look at the relationship between men and women, going so far as to offer tips on how to make a marriage work, and how to avoid sexual boredom within matrimony. Father Bardecki, Wojtyla's friend from the Kraków Catholic newspaper, says

Wojtyla sent him an early draft of the book and asked him for his comments. The elder priest was stunned by what he read. "It's not an easy book. It deals with issues between men and women that many priests would rather try and avoid. Remember books published in Poland were subject to censorship. I knew someone in the censor's office who told me they were absolutely aghast that a priest would write a book like this. When word got out in advance of publication that Wojtyla had written a bold book, he got scared and wanted to take it back. I convinced him not to do that, but rather to go ahead with its publication." The book became a best-seller in Poland and was later translated into half a dozen languages.

When Wojtyla returned to Poland at the end of the Council's first session, in December of that year, he knew that a major decision about his future was imminent. Archbishop Eugeniusz Baziak of Kraków, who had succeeded Sapieha and with whom Wojtyla worked closely, had died in June, and Wojtyla had been asked to fill in temporarily. The Polish government and the Catholic Church hierarchy were locked in a test of wills over whether state approval was needed to name bishops, and until it was resolved, the post of archbishop would remain officially vacant.

As was so often the case, the Communist authorities in this instance demonstrated that they did not have the stomach for a protracted struggle, and agreed that the Church alone would be responsible for naming its leaders. It was a concession that would be regretted bitterly, all the way to the inner sanctums of the Kremlin, in 1978.

Meanwhile, in May 1963, Wojtyla, in his capacity as acting head of the archdiocese, carried out one of his more pleasant duties and drove to the border town of Cieszyn to greet an august visitor, Franz Cardinal König, archbishop of Vienna. So

VATICAN II

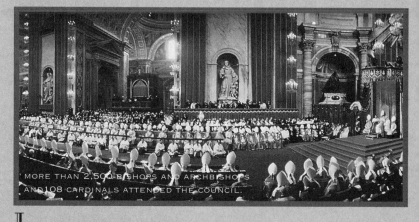

MORE THAN 2,500 BISHOPS AND ARCHBISHOPS AND 108 CARDINALS ATTENDED THE COUNCIL.

It is no small thing to call together the entire hierarchy of a universal church, but Pope John XXIII did not hesitate to do so within months of his election in 1958. He knew, or at least sensed, that the Catholic Church was unprepared to deal with the modern world and, like any good chief executive, wanted to make sure his top lieutenants were all working together to achieve his goals.

There had been numerous ecumenical councils called by previous popes, but few of such magnitude. The Council of Nicaea was convoked by Constantine in 325 as a way of settling the dispute between rival groups over the relationship between God the Father and God the Son, the First and Second Persons of the Blessed Trinity.

When the Church was under serious threat by the various Protestant reformation movements, Pope Paul III decided in 1545 to bring together his senior advisers to devise a response. The Council of Trent's work was so extensive that it lasted not only through Paul's pontificate but also those of his two immediate successors, Julius III and Pius IV. By the time the Council of Trent completed its work in 1563, it had reorganized many of the Church's procedures for marriage, Holy Orders, and the role of the Church in interpreting and promoting the teaching of the Bible.

The First Vatican Council was convened in 1869 by Pius IX to come to terms with the concept of papal infallibility. This was the first council to draw on the wisdom of such a large group of churchmen: More than seven hundred bishops attended the fourteen general sessions. Among the topics debated were the oneness of God, the literal interpretation of God as creator of all things, the sanctity of Holy Scripture, and the recognition of miracles as proof of God's grace. The First Vatican Council might have lasted longer if the armies of King Victor Emmanuel II of Italy had not stormed Rome and confiscated the Papal States.

Against this historical background, John XXIII decided in January 1959 that it was time to bring his Church up to date with the twentieth century. The pope had been in office only three months when plans for the Council were made public. Organizing the Council and ensuring that it would focus on the work the Holy Father wanted done took three years. Those who attended were divided into thirteen commissions, each of which concentrated on specific questions to be debated.

The work list of the Council was, by the ponderous yardstick of Church bureaucracy, mindboggling. Most American Catholics will remember it as the event that resulted in Masses being said in English, the priest facing the congregation, the end of compulsorily meatless Fridays, and a new tolerance for and spirit of collaboration with other faiths. From the Church's point of view, Vatican II was a complete new beginning in its way of viewing its work. It adopted a new constitution of dogma, which recognized the role the Church has in carrying out Christ's wishes; a constitution on sacred liturgy, which put new emphasis on the participation by worshipers instead of just the priest; a decree on ecumenism, which opened the way for new overtures to other Christian denominations; another declaration, that stated categorically that the Church wanted to improve relations with non-Christian faiths; and a declaration on religious freedom, which pointed out the dignity of the individual and the right to worship.

The effects of the Council are still being debated. Traditionalists such as Archbishop Marcel LeFebvre insisted that it was all a mistake that should be undone to restore the Church's unique position. The majority of the Church hierarchy, including Bishop Wojtyla, embraced the changes and saw that the Church had to join the rest of the world, or be left out of its progress. And John Paul II has led that participation through the closing years of the century.

genuine and friendly was the welcome he received that the Austrian decided Wojtyla was a man worth watching. For the second time in his life—the first being his welcoming speech to Sapieha as a schoolboy in Wadowice—Wojtyla's courtesy and Christian humility would catch the eye of a powerful prince of the Church who took a subsequent interest in him, this time conveying his favorable impression to Cardinal Wyszynski in Warsaw. The church's senior statesmen, however, had bigger matters in minds. In June, John XXIII died and was replaced by Paul VI. He quickly affirmed his intention to carry on with the work of the Council, and Wojtyla and his fellow bishops returned to Rome later in the year, where the man from Kraków continued to impress his colleagues. In December 1963 Wyszynski nominated the forty-three-year-old Wojtyla to the post of archbishop, an appointment approved by Pope Paul. Fifteen years later, Vienna's König would play a key role when he recommended—indeed, championed—Wojtyla as the man to lead the Church through the closing years of the century.

If Wojtyla was a more combative bishop than he had been a priest to the Communist authorities in Poland, he became an even more serious and formidable opponent as an archbishop. His resourcefulness was unending and confounding. While attending the Vatican Council, he broadcast reports on its progress, and his own activities, back to Poland on Vatican Radio. He never hesitated to comment on events back home for those who might not otherwise hear about them in the state-controlled media. As a negotiator, he was particularly difficult to deal with, since he knew the philosophical underpinnings of Marxism better than did many of the party officials who were sent out to tame him. He continued to organize Polish Catholics along lines that emphasized their membership in the universal

Wojtyla's consecration as cardinal by Pope Paul VI, 1967.

Church, while minimizing or ignoring completely the restrictive role that the state played in their lives.

The example par excellence of his persistent sparring with the regime was the Church at Nowa Huta, a Kraków industrial suburb that had been founded as an example of the socialist ideal—a workingman's paradise. Naturally, the Communists did not plan on building a church for Nowa Huta. Wojtyla insisted, and when permission was initially refused, planted a cross on the site where he wanted the church and said Mass there, in the open air. He demanded permits to stage public processions on every major religious feast day, and when they were initially denied, demanded to know why. Lacking any justifiable reason, the local authorities caved in, bolstering the bishop's reputation as someone who could successfully face them down.

Thus it was more than just a bureaucratic victory when in

NOWA HUTA

The name of the town, meaning New Foundry, was no more imaginative than its physical layout. Straight streets, poorly paved roads, and plain apartment blocks announced to its inhabitants and the world at large that this was a place where work was meant to be done. Nowa Huta, was meant to be a prime example of the new socialist towns that the Communist leadership intended to seed throughout its empire. With the heavy destruction that Poland suffered during World War II, the need for new communities was obvious. But the Communists' idea of a place to live had little to do with comfort or contentment.

The town, with a population of two hundred thousand, was built on the edge of Kraków, and was a "company town" in the strictest sense—no one would live there who didn't work there. And there was only one place to work: the Nowa Huta steel plant. Belching fumes and sparks from its mammoth smokestacks, Nowa Huta was a living, working Hades. Its employees and their families were expected to make their purchases locally, travel only when the worker's schedule permitted it, and stay out of trouble. And trouble included practicing their faith, Roman Catholicism. Those who insisted on going to Mass had to walk for two and a half hours to get to the nearest church.

Despite repeated efforts by the Kraków archdiocese, permission for construction of a church was consistently denied. There would be, said the authorities, no church in this new socialist town. But they had not counted on an opponent like Archbishop Wojtyla. From the time of his appointment as auxiliary bishop of Kraków, the young prelate was pushing the communists to let the workers of Nowa Huta have their own place of worship.

During the 1960s, residents of Nowa Huta began the ingenious—and to the regime, outrageous—practice of erecting makeshift chapels overnight, where Mass would be said at dawn as workers trooped to their shifts at the steel mill. By noontime the police had knocked the buildings down, only to find a new one in its place the next day.

Wojtyla's contribution to the crusade for a church provided early evidence of his persistence and his taste for high-visibility conflict. Each week, the young bishop would renew his inquiry about the status of the archdiocese's request to build a church in Nowa Huta. And each week he would be told that the permit, though not denied, had still not been authorized. Wojtyla decided to test his opponents' mettle. He planted the crozier, or staff, that identified him as a bishop, into the spot where the church was meant to be built. It is here, he said, and, consecrating the spot, began to say Mass in the open air. Such activities infuriated the Communists, but never to the point where they took action against the upstart.

Finally, in 1967, permission was granted, without explanation, to build a church in Nowa Huta. Wojtyla was elated, but knew better than to celebrate too soon. Steady harassment—shortage of construction materials, loss of important shipping orders, torturously slow approval of safety permits and inspection reports—by the authorities dragged out construction for a decade. When at last it was ready, it was not Archbishop Wojtyla but Cardinal Wojtyla who consecrated the modernistic, soaring structure, where a crucified Christ arches painfully against three metal spikes driven directly into the church's walls.

Wojtyla had less than a year to enjoy the sight of the finished church before he was elected to the papacy. But he returned, joyfully, on his second visit as pope in 1983, to conse-

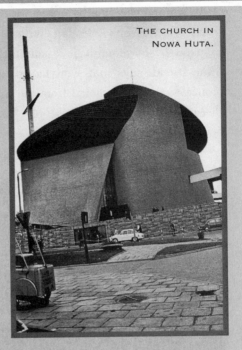

THE CHURCH IN NOWA HUTA.

crate a second church in Nowa Huta. More than a million people turned out to hear and see the native son.

With the end of communism, Nowa Huta became just another small town with a huge and inefficient industrial enterprise that could not compete according to the new rules of the marketplace. Having overcome totalitarian government, officially sanctioned harassment, and grinding poverty, the workers faced a new threat to their welfare that not even John Paul could help them prevent: layoffs.

1967 ground was finally broken for the Nowa Huta church on Karl Marx Avenue. Stefan Wilkanowicz, an editor of the Kraków-based monthly publication *ZNAC*, and another long-time friend, says that Wojtyla took pleasure not just in the concessions he extracted from the authorities but also in the lesson it imparted to the people. "As bishop of Kraków, he symbolized the primacy of moral over state power."

He also knew how to administer his archdiocese. When he convened a synod, or convention of all the priests and interested laymen in the Kraków region, Wilkanowicz, who was a member of its main commission, recalls that Wojtyla presided over it like an experienced executive, not like a remarkable young man in a powerful post. "He used small group discussions to get everyone involved, and he would move from group to group, listening, commenting, encouraging them. He had the process completely under control, but he wasn't authoritarian in any way. It was excellent preparation for a future pope."

The Church is an institution that well-wishers might describe as chatty, detractors as gossip-ridden. Reports about the man in Poland who was experiencing such success against the Communists, who was a published author and certified intellectual began to make their way along the informal grapevine that functions as the Vatican's in-house publicity organ. When Paul was developing his strategy of trying to come to terms with the Soviet Union and its allies' antireligious tendencies, he consulted with as many bishops and cardinals who lived behind the Iron Curtain as possible. Wojtyla, whom the Polish experts on Church affairs had hoped might be more malleable than the older Primate Wyszynski, was frequently permitted to travel to Rome for these consultations, and, within the walls of the Vatican, became something of a quasi-permanent visitor. To the outside world, and especially in the West, he was a nonentity, another poor Pole downtrodden by the crushing curse of communism. But Paul, who had once served as a Vatican diplomat in Poland, better understood the younger man's true worth. In May 1967, at age forty-seven, Karol Wojtyla was named a cardinal by Pope Paul; two months later, he was consecrated by the pontiff and received the red skullcap that signified his exalted office. The ceremony took place in the Sistine Chapel, where, as a newly invested cardinal, Wojtyla would take part in the next papal conclave to elect Paul's successor.

1969

CHAPTER FIVE

THE ROAD TO ROME

Modestly, quietly, but becoming increasingly famous within the Vatican, Wojtyla learned to mute his instinctive loathing of communism at home to spare his people its excesses. The year 1968 was one in which countries everywhere seemed to be trying to evolve from old rules that no longer served new realities. Students in Germany, France, Italy, Mexico, and all across the United States were rebelling against the values that had governed their parents' lives. Poland and other countries in Eastern Europe expressed similar pent-up frustrations with the confines of socialism. When student riots broke out in Warsaw in 1968, Wojtyla and Wyszynski worked together behind the scenes to keep them from getting out of hand. Their decision for restraint and the timing of their call for caution were exactly right. In July of that year, Soviet tanks and troops flooded Poland's neighbor to the south, Czechoslovakia, to put a definitive end to the

"Prague spring" of liberalization experiments overseen by Alexander Dubcek. The invasion of Czechoslovakia sent a chill through the Eastern bloc and signaled unmistakably that reform was not in the cards as long as the masters in Moscow had enough troops and the will to use them.

Even in those days, however, Wojtyla saw weaknesses in the Communist system that self-proclaimed experts could not. Within his archdiocese, the regime found it difficult to muzzle the ever-growing, always changing variety of Church-related activities he cooked up. He ran programs for schoolchildren, for youth groups, for university students, and for prospective priests in seminaries.

The constant stream of ideas came from the wide range of contacts and friends whom Wojtyla tapped in Kraków. His skill as an administrator and pastor to his city was matched by the almost laserlike attention he could muster during conversations. Friends from all periods of his life agree: Wojtyla knew how to listen. He and Stefan Wilkanowicz, the editor of *ZNAC*, would have a monthly meal during which the cardinal would probe his friend for smidgens of intelligence: What are people saying? What are they concerned about? What frightens them? "He was not constrained in any way," Wilkanowicz recalls. "He listened, then responded, and that led to a deeper level of discussion. His ability to concentrate totally on what was being said to him was phenomenal. He got every last bit of information out of everyone he talked to. The only problem with that was that he couldn't bear for a conversation to be over, so he was always late for each subsequent appointment."

Wojtyla was working as many as twenty hours a day in his job as cardinal—at precisely the point in his life when he might have imagined he had risen as far as he could hope in the Church. Did he have ambition to ascend that last final step, to be the 263rd successor to Peter, to lead the world's oldest kingdom?

❧　❧　❧

"He had no premonition of what was in store for him."

His Polish friends staunchly deny such suggestions. "He had no premonition of what was in store for him," insists Father Suder, the parish priest at the church in Wadowice across from Wojtyla's birthplace. "He wanted to spend his life in Kraków, studying and writing," avers Father Bardecki, the *Tygodnik Powszechny* editor.

Wojtyla's actions tell a different story. Aware of Pope Paul's fondness of him, he began making more frequent trips to Rome, where he often saw the pontiff for private conversations—rare gestures of honor in the stuffy bureaucracy of the Vatican. It can only be speculated upon, but it is not difficult to imagine why Paul, a man tortured throughout his papacy by indecision and self-doubt, felt affection for the outgoing, smiling, confident young Polish superstar. Unkind Vatican voices dubbed Paul "Amleto"—Hamlet—for his inability to make up his mind on the major issues confronting him.

None was more controversial than the Church's stand on birth control. Technological advances in preventing pregnancy called into question the Church's centuries-old teaching that the main purpose of marriage is procreation (sex outside of marriage was and still is considered an occasion of

Karol Cardinal Wojtyla performs an outdoor Mass in Kraków, after his investiture, 1967.

sin). Wojtyla's book, *Love and Responsibility*, was considered a bombshell, in part because he wrote that married couples can and could try to make each other happy in all ways—including sexually—without guilt or embarrassment as long as they demonstrated respect for each other. While such a mild concession to physical pleasure may seem hopelessly outdated in the age of unbounded sexuality, it was innovative language in Poland and elsewhere in the early 1960s, especially when coming from a clergyman.

Paul, fully aware of what was going on in the world around him, was trapped between two unpalatable positions. He could rescind previous Church teaching, most recently elaborated by Pius XI in an encyclical, or letter, from the pope to the Church's bishops and priests, in which he lays out official Catholic teaching on matters of relevance. In that encyclical, Pius decisively rejected the notion that artificial contraception could be employed. While contemporary reality would make it easy, even logical, for Paul to point out the advances in science and the threat of overpopulation as grounds for permitting birth control, the responsibility for, and implications of, reversing the decisions of his predecessors weighed Paul down. On the other hand, the need to keep the Church current with changing times was the stated purpose of convening the Second Vatican Council, which had a mandate to review all aspects of Church teaching.

Popes are absolute monarchs, but that does not mean that they are free of accountability. On the contrary, they believe they are responsible, directly, to the highest authority—Jesus Christ, who founded the Catholic Church and left it in the hands of his trusted apostle Peter. The Church's Magisterium, or authority to teach the faithful, comes from an unbroken line of authority. The responsibility vested in a pontiff for interpreting Christ's teachings is incalculable. And none of the pope's powers is more open to dissent than his ability to speak infallibly. The Church limits the pope's right to speak without

Questions of life and death are not easily resolved. Yet the obligation to deal with them is part of the price of power, and power is a function few popes are shy about exercising. It was a cruel irony that the task of releasing *Humanae Vitae*, the 1968 encyclical on artificial birth control that split the Catholic Church, fell to Paul VI, the tortured Milanese for whom any decision was wrenching, let alone one about so controversial a topic.

As with the Vatican Council, Paul was following through on an initiative of his immediate predecessor, John XXIII, who in 1961 had ordered a commission of clerics and lay specialists to examine the questions around artificial contraception. Though various means of preventing birth had been used for centuries, the rapidly evolving technology—especially the birth control pill—had convinced John that the Church must have up-to-date information on which to base its positions, even if those positions did not change as a result.

Paul waited to hear from the experts. Yet when they spoke, they did not tell him what he wanted to hear. Instead, in a scholarly report submitted in June 1966, they concluded that there was nothing defin-

itive in the Bible to prevent Catholics from using birth control. In retrospect, it is obvious that Paul would have preferred the commission to report back just the opposite. Yet he was unable to bring himself to reject the findings boldly. Instead, he pondered—for two full years—before overruling his own experts and releasing *Humanae Vitae*.

The document is widely perceived in the United States as an antifeminist tract, written by a celibate and elderly man who knew nothing about the demands of love. Certainly Paul lacked female input in preparing his encyclical, and he had no personal experience in the matters of which he was writing. He anticipated that his words would provoke criticism, though perhaps he was unprepared for the magnitude of furor. Still, he made no apology for what he had decided, and early in the encyclical he stated clearly that it was his work alone. "We could not regard as definitive and requiring unequivocal acceptance the conclusions arrived at by the commission," he wrote. "They were not such as to exempt Us from the duty of examining personally this serious question. Now that We have sifted carefully the evidence sent to Us and intently studied the whole matter, as well as prayed constantly to God, We, by virtue of the mandate entrusted to Us by Christ, intend to give Our reply to this series of grave questions."

The answers were not at all to the liking of most American Catholics. Paul had never intended to make it easier for Catholics—men or women, married or single—to have sex without consequences. He was aware that the population of the world was growing rapidly, but concluded that it was more important to protect the dignity of humankind than the ability of the earth to support its inhabitants. The decision of whether to have children, Paul argues, must be made by men and women fully aware that if they do engage in sex, they are likely to produce children.

With unflinching condemnation, Paul went on to list the forms of artificial birth control he ruled unacceptable. The strongest language was reserved for abortion, but he made clear that the emerging technology of birth control devices and processes were also sinful.

Paul knew the outcry his decision would bring. In *Humanae Vitae* he wrote: "Some people today raise the objection against this particular doctrine of the Church concerning the moral laws governing marriage, that human intelligence has both the right and the responsibility to control those forces of irrational nature that come within its ambit and to direct them toward ends beneficial to man. Others ask whether it is not reasonable to use artificial birth control if by so doing, the harmony and peace of a family are better served and more suitable conditions are provided for the education of children already born. To this question we must give a clear reply."

He then proceeded to show that for all his cloistered years, he was aware of what went on in the outside world. "Not much experience is needed to understand that men—and especially the young, who are so exposed to temptation—need incentives to keep the moral law, and it is an evil thing to make it easy for them to break that law. A man who grows accustomed to the use of contraceptive methods may forget the reverence due to a woman, and reduce her to being a mere instrument for the satisfaction of his own desires, no longer considering her as his partner whom he should surround with care and affection."

The effect of *Humanae Vitae* was to alienate generations of Catholics, especially in the developed world, and to label the Church an anachronistic institution. A close reading of the encyclical, however, reveals that it was not only insightful but also prophetic.

question of error to matters of doctrinal truth, not biblical interpretation or of discipline.

Of course, the Bible—which is the primary source of knowledge about Christ's time on earth—says nothing specifically about birth control pills or other technical devices to prevent conception, since they did not exist. Thus Paul, a diffident pastor by nature, found himself in the impossible position of having to decide an issue that would inevitably outrage and possibly drive away a large portion of his flock.

Paul did not want to deal with the divisive issue; it was thrust on him when he inherited the work of the Second Vatican Council from John XXIII. First Paul appointed a mixed committee of clergymen and scientific and ethical scholars, who concluded that Scripture contained no specific condemnation of birth control. Then a commission of theological experts was asked to assess the issue. One of its members was the then archbishop of Kraków, Karol Wojtyla. Never one to shy away from the complicated aspects of human existence—and sex must certainly rank among those—Wojtyla had unabashedly studied human sexuality and conducted frank discussions with married couples in his diocese over the years all of which contributed toward the creation of *Love and Responsibility*. His longtime friend, Father Malinski, recalls that Wojtyla would probe the young people who came to him with questions and problems about their sexuality. His questions, Malinski says, could be direct to the point of embarrassing. He wanted to know what caused them to be aroused, how they demonstrated their love for one another, the role that sex played in their marriage, what kind of things could cause them to think about ending their relationship, if they regarded the commitment they had made to each other to be lasting, binding for life. The priest listened, carefully as always, without making judgments on what

With John Cardinal Krol of Philadelphia during a visit to the United States, 1969.

he was hearing. It was a kind of love he would never know, and yet he insisted on knowing about it.

Wojtyla believed that while he himself was celibate, it was important for him to be able to understand the emotions and problems that the faithful encountered. But because he was interested in understanding those problems did not mean that he took a permissive or casual attitude toward the issue of personal morality. As he would demonstrate years later as pope, Wojtyla believed that all aspects of human behavior—selfishness, suffering, sexual drive, and ambition, among others—were windows of opportunity for the greater glory of God. His deeply imbedded mysticism, drawn in part from the writings and example of St. John of the Cross and Wojtyla's late friend Jan Tyranowski, convinced him of the validity of the notion that redemption and salvation could be attained through suffering. Thus it was not as an unfeeling celibate that Wojtyla believed married couples who did not want children should simply refrain from having sex. Abstinence was, in his view, another opportunity for them—and furthermore, one denied him and other single people—to bear hardship as a means of worship.

This deeply held creed only further cemented his relationship with Paul, who, despite all the advice and conclusions of his expert panels, had deep misgivings about authorizing so radical a change in the magisterium. Rather than allow the Vatican Council to debate and, in essence, vote on the question of permitting birth control, Paul removed it from the agenda and announced that he personally would listen to the evidence and make a determination. For an incredible four years, from 1964 to 1968, Paul convened one commission after the other, listened to its conclusions, then dismissed its members and turned to yet another group of experts for advice. Though no one knew it at the time, it seems obvious now that what Paul wanted to be told was to do nothing. Once it became clear that the commission of which Wojtyla was a member was moving toward an implicit endorsement of birth control, Wojtyla selectively avoided attending its most important sessions, including the one where its members signed their names to the final document.

Paul's decision to continue the ban on any forms of artificial contraception was contained in *Humanae Vitae*, released in July 1968. Its practical effect was to polarize the Catholic Church in Western Europe and North America, to lead millions to stop attending Mass or leave the Church altogether, while the majority of those who stayed simply ignored the pope's warning that to use birth control devices was a grave sin. While Paul honestly believed that he was defending the dignity of human life and interpreting God's law in the most honest way possible, he also knew that his decision had caused millions to lose their faith, and he agonized over the consequences of his action. He never wrote another encyclical.

One supporter was Karol Wojtyla. He not only spoke in favor of *Humanae Vitae*, he also praised the pope for having the courage to put the value of human life over the considerations of modern-day morals. To encourage the men and women who were the ones most directly affected, he organized discussion groups in his diocese to help couples live by its strictures. For the lonely man in the Vatican, the value of the enthusiastic loyalty he received from the cardinal of Kraków was inestimable.

Wojtyla was also expanding his contacts and his profile throughout the world during his tenure as cardinal. He traveled to Australia, New Zealand, New Guinea, Canada, and on two occasions, the United States. In 1969 he visited, among other cities, Philadelphia, where he got to know John Cardinal Krol, a Polish American who would later, along with König of Vienna, be one of the main forces behind the election of the first Polish pope.

With Pope Paul VI in Rome.

Wojtyla was often away in Rome or on other foreign trips in the 1970s. But that did not mean that nothing was happening in Poland. Riots once again erupted, this time in Gdansk, in December 1970, when the government tried to raise food prices. When workers went on strike and then poured into the streets, army troops were called out and fired on civilians, killing dozens. The prime minister, Wladyslaw Gomulka, was deposed for permitting the situation to get out of hand. Both Wojtyla and Cardinal Wyszynski urged restraint, but for the cardinal in Kraków, the regime's response was yet another indication that Communists could be, and in fact should be, dealt with firmly.

There were more riots in 1976, again after a rise in food prices, but the prime minister, Edward Gierek, took a conciliatory line this time, canceling the increases and forbidding police or soldiers from using deadly force. It was a major step back from the authoritarian style of rule that the Soviet Union favored in its allied countries, and no blood was shed. Still, the 1976 disturbances gave birth to the first organized effort to unite Polish workers in a way that would give them protection against the government. A few years later, the movement, refined and more widespread, would become Solidarity.

Wojtyla, meanwhile, had been accorded a singular honor by Paul VI: He was asked to conduct series of meditations for the Holy Father's Lenten retreat in Rome. Rather than adapt any of his previous writings, Wojtyla chose to create an entirely new piece of work to present to the pontiff. His friend Father Malinski remembers the tremendous efforts that went into the series of sermons. "He went to Zakopane [a nearby ski resort] and cut himself off from the world so he could fashion it as quickly as possible. It was very cold, but I learned later that some of the time he wrote lying prostrate on the floor of the chapel where he was praying and working."

Wojtyla had decided to take a bold approach to this once-in-a-lifetime opportunity. He, along with the rest of the world, knew that Paul was ill and, as always, insecure. The howl of protest following the publication of *Humanae Vitae* had stung the pontiff beyond any chance of recovery. Paul had done what his conscience told him, and was being made to pay the price.

And that, in effect, is what Wojtyla said in his sermons, later published under the title *A Sign of Contradiction*. The pope was the personification of the contradiction of which he spoke. Paul's decision, while undeniably taken in defense of human life, and therefore for the best of motives, was being condemned

Pope John Paul I was pope a mere 33 days.

because it made contemporary life more difficult for Catholics. It was a criticism Wojtyla himself would hear about his own papacy, which would begin in fewer than three years.

Paul died of a heart attack on August 6, 1978. He had reigned for fifteen years, completed the work of the Vatican Council his predecessor started, been the first pope to fly in an airplane and to visit the Holy Land from Rome, fashioned the Church's first concerted effort to deal with communism, and sent its liberal wing into revolt with his refusal to permit birth control.

The Catholic Church was ready for a change of leadership.

Wojtyla was taking part in his first conclave to elect a pope, the 263rd. He and Wyszynski arrived in Rome a week after Paul's death. The buzzword among the cardinals who would choose the next pope was "pastoral." They wanted someone who had experience in dealing with people and their problems. Paul had been brilliant in many ways, but his career had consisted of a series of diplomatic and administrative jobs. What the church needed now was someone to give its policies a human face, to put into practice the reforms and modernization that Vatican II had commissioned.

There were those who thought it might be time to look outside the circle of Italian cardinals who had monopolized the papacy since 1523. Wojtyla was known to have been one of Paul's favorite cardinals, but in the spirit of mournful gloom and the oppressive Roman heat in which the electors gathered, that was not necessarily a good thing. Nevertheless, the Kraków cardinal did receive some votes on the first two ballots, when no clear winner was declared. On the third round of voting, the cardinals elected Albino Luciani, the patriarch of Venice, an affable man whose self-deprecating manner and ready smile seemed exactly what was needed after the dry, dour reign of Paul. As a sign of respect for his two immediate predecessors, who had overseen the momentous changes brought about by Vatican II, Luciani chose to reign under the double name John Paul.

Unfortunately, Luciani, who had suffered from tuberculosis as a young man, was never in good health. He died in his sleep thirty-three days after being elected, apparently of a heart attack.

The search for a vigorous leader who would take the Church into the new millennium resumed, this time with a certain desperation.

1979

CHAPTER SIX

MAN FROM A FARAWAY LAND

Perhaps not even Wojtyla himself would be able to answer with complete certainty what he felt as he attended his second conclave in three months. The mythology that has grown up around the pope is concentrated in the notion that his election was a complete surprise. There is, to be sure, circumstantial evidence to indicate that Wojtyla expected to be back in Poland soon. The cardinal packed only one bag for the trip to Rome, had made a round-trip airplane reservation, signaling that he intended to return to Kraków, and advised photographers asking him to pose for pictures to save their film—he would not be the next pope. In all this, Wojtyla was acting in obedience to a piece of cynical Roman wisdom about conclaves: "He who goes in pope will come out a cardinal." The witticism aptly captures the conflicting emotions of ambition and humility that contribute to the election of a pontiff. To be perceived as openly running for the job is usually a fatal blow to a man's chances. Polite demurrals and frequent references to the will of God take the place of stump speeches.

Rather than campaigning, those who are considered *papabili*—possible popes—strive to have their names come up, artlessly, in the confidential conversations that take place among the voting members of the College of Cardinals. Since he had been closely associated with Paul, worked for the winning side in the intense debate that led to publication of *Humanae Vitae*, delivered the masterful set of sermons during the late pope's Lenten retreat, and built up a considerable number of acquaintances and contacts in his international travels, Wojtyla was a natural topic of speculation among his peers.

He was not, however, considered one of the likely candidates, as handicapped by the self-styled Vatican experts and the journalists who descend in hordes on St. Peter's every time a pope dies. The two favorites going into the conclave were the same Italian cardinals tipped at the August gathering that produced John Paul I: Giovanni Benelli of Florence and Giuseppe Siri of Genoa. Benelli was regarded as a moderate-to-liberal influence, which in Vatican terms meant that he could be counted on to continue the Vatican Council policies of making the Church relevant in the modern world. Siri, by contrast, was considered a conservative who, while paying the required lip service to the Council, would use his papacy to retard or rescind much of its work. It was said that he had been a contender for the papacy at the conclave earlier in the year, but Benelli had been instrumental in blocking Siri in favor of John Paul I. The different philosophies of Siri and Benelli represented perfectly the polarization that the Council had brought about. Among Catholics, and especially among the clergy whose lives were devoted to the Church, there was a genuine split of opinion about the need for change. Why, some asked, should the traditional Latin Mass be sacrificed and replaced by the local language? Others would ask the obverse: What was wrong with hearing Mass in one's own tongue, so that all its parts could be understood by the faithful? The emphasis on ecumenism and the reaching out to other faiths to find what they had in common with Catholicism was also a topic of debate. Some Catholics felt it was high time to try to bridge the gaps that separated them from fellow Christians. Others insisted that if the Catholic Church did not rigorously maintain its ideological purity, it would become indistinguishable from the Protestant sects.

There was also embarrassment at the absurdly short time John Paul I had ruled. His feeble health and quick death reinforced the notion that the Church leadership was made up of doddering old men who spent their lives behind cloistered walls and who understood little of the world around them. None of the cardinals who were gathering in Rome that October would say it directly, but they were looking this time for a leader who would project an image of vigor.

Siri and Benelli apparently had roughly equal numbers of supporters going into the conclave. As it turned out, that approximate parity convinced some of the cardinals that neither would prevail and that another candidate would have to be found.

In retrospect, Wojtyla seems an obvious choice. His intellectual credentials were impressive, his range of contacts was extensive, he knew a good deal about the workings of the Vatican because of the number of trips he had made there, yet the bulk of his career had been spent in pastoral endeavors. He spoke several languages, and he knew firsthand about the Communist world, with which the Church realized it would have to deal in the coming years.

But Wojtyla was not an Italian, and in the climate of 1978, that seemed an impossible barrier. The last non-Italian pope had been Adrian VI, a Dutchman elected on January 9, 1522. He died on September 14 of the next year, but not before thoroughly alienating the Roman populace. They considered him a heathen; he looked at their relaxed way of life as debauched. Whether true or not, the story is told that Adrian ordered the frescoes painted by Michelangelo in the Sistine Chapel to be whitewashed because he found the naked bodies objectionable. (The order was never carried out.) More seriously, Adrian failed to understand the gravity of a challenge to his authority by a German monk named Martin Luther. Adrian's short, uninspiring reign gave non-Italians a bad name in papal politics; the so-called Dutch curse that would not be shaken for more than four hundred years.

But as they surveyed the possibilities, the cardinals arriving for the October 1978 conclave were coming to the conclusion that it was time to look beyond Italy. One who was more than willing to have a "foreign" pope was Franz Cardinal König, from Vienna. Too old himself to be considered, he began bruiting the name of the young cardinal from Kraków who had the intellect of a philosopher, a common touch that made him popular with the faithful, and an outstanding track record of dealing in a tough yet diplomatic manner with the Communist authorities in his homeland. The other Wojtyla cheerleader was John Cardinal Krol of Philadelphia, of Polish heritage himself, who had met Wojtyla during the Kraków cardinal's tour of the United States. Quietly, in a way that would not produce any backlash, they began floating their candidate's name.

Wojtyla, it appears, steered clear of any preconclave gossip groups. Instead he spent time in prayer at the Polish College, where he was staying prior to the conclave, or with two Polish bishops who were stationed in Rome, Bishop Rubin and Bishop Deskur, the latter of whom was paralyzed by a stroke the day before the conclave was to begin. During the intervening days, he made visits to Lake Vico and the papal retreat Castel Gandolfo. Wojtyla no doubt knew that his name was being bandied about, but was either powerless or unwilling to do anything about it. When he turned up for the voting, directly from visiting his friend Deskur at the hospital, he had with him a Marxist philosophical journal that he intended to read while the voting was carried out.

The 111 cardinals who would vote in the conclave met in the Sistine Chapel for the first session on Sunday, October 15, 1978. To be elected, a candidate would need 75 votes, or two-thirds of the ballots cast. Benelli and Siri were, predictably, the leaders after the first round, but it was obvious that neither would be able to muster the required number. They were canceling each other out, and in so doing, eliminating the prospect that any Italian might be elected. Though they remained the front-runners throughout four ballots on Sunday, it was clear that neither was electable. Behind the scenes, the manuvering intesified as black smoke poured forth from the chimney above the chapel, the traditional signal to the faithful waiting outside in St. Peter's Square that the voting had not produced a winner.

The cardinals dined together that night before retiring to the Vatican cells in which they were to be sequestered until a new pope was selected. Since conclave proceedings are guarded by secrecy, it is impossible to know who said what to whom, but by Monday, October 16, talk of alternatives was sweeping the electors. The three men reportedly most discussed were all non-Italian: Along with Wojtyla were Dutch

Johannes Cardinal Willebrands and Argentinian Eduardo Cardinal Pironio. Wojtyla received a number of votes during that day's first round, an even larger total during the next balloting, the second of that day and the sixth of the conclave overall. By that point, König and Krol knew that their informal pep talks of the previous days were paying off. Another round of voting was inconclusive; then, in the eighth round, the toll for Wojtyla began its slow, inexorable rise. As it passed the magic number of 75, Wojtyla, it is said, blushed deeply, and began furiously scrawling on a piece of paper the first words he would utter as pope. That story, if true, might indicate that he had had no premonition that he would be elected that day. But it is unlikely that he was caught by surprise. His friends König and Krol (who died in 1996) obviously had told him of their politicking on his behalf. The number of votes cast for him had been rising with each ballot. Astute politician that he was, he must have seen the trend was moving in his direction. In the end, he is believed to have captured 94 of the votes. Whether that number included his own ballot will never be known. The pieces of paper on which the candidates' names are written are burned immediately afterward to protect the conclave's secrecy.

The post-election ritual of pope making is one of the most impressive coronation ceremonies still left, the more so because the faithful in the world at large do not know immediately who has been chosen to lead them. Wojtyla was taken to a small room off the Sistine Chapel and fitted with the white vestments that only a pope may wear. Three sizes are kept in readiness—small, medium, and large—to accommodate the new pontiff, whatever his height and girth. Then he was led back into the chapel to receive each of the 110 other cardinals who had taken part in the voting.

Inauguration of Pope John Paul II, October 22, 1978.

❧ ❧ ❧

"Habemus papam."

By then, white smoke had risen from the chimney above the Sistine Chapel, so the crowd filling St. Peter's Square knew there was a pope. About twenty-five minutes after he had been declared the winner, Karol Józef Wojtyla stood behind closed doors, poised to walk out onto the loggia, the main balcony above the doors of St. Peter's Basilica. On the other side of the doors, which blocked Wojtyla from the view of the throng below, Pericle Cardinal Felici, the senior cardinal among those voting, drew out the traditional announcement, prolonging the suspense: *"Habemus papam* (We have a pope). *Karolum Cardinalem"*—another long pause—*"Wojtyla."* He would reign, Felici told the crowd, as Pope John Paul II.

The overwhelmingly Roman crowd's reaction was one of stunned puzzlement. Who did he say? What name was that? Not one of ours. It must be a foreigner. But which foreigner? An African? A Japanese? Finally, the mystery was solved. The Pole!

A few seconds later, Wojtyla, wearing the white skullcap, called a *zucchetto* in Italian, and robe of his new office, appeared on the loggia and waited for the roar to diminish. Although he made it seem spontaneous, his first words to the crowd standing beneath him were crucial. The last non-Italian pope had been despised by the Romans, who actually celebrated when he died. Wojtyla was much too astute to possibly alienate the crowd. So he delivered his remarks not in Latin— which, though it is the official language of the Church, is one which few people speak fluently—but in Italian. His command of the language was almost perfect, and he accentuated that fact precisely by calling it into question. "I do not know if I will be able to explain myself in your—our—Italian language. If I make a mistake you will correct me." This was brilliant stage strategy by the practiced actor. First of all, he used the simple "I" instead of the "we" employed by popes in the past to signify their position as a monarch. Then he won the crowd's sympathy immediately by claiming not to speak the language well, although he clearly did. Third, by pointedly correcting himself, and switching from the use of "your" to "our," he made clear that as of the moment of his election, he considered himself part of Italy. Finally, he asked the crowd to correct him—he, the supreme pontiff, the Vicar of Christ, the leader of the Roman Catholic Church—if he made a grammatical mistake. The effect was immediate and overwhelming. They loved him.

Avila, Spain, 1982

CHAPTER SEVEN

SERVANT OF THE SERVANTS OF GOD

It was not just the Romans. For a while, it seemed the whole world had caught John Paul mania. After a decade and a half of dour and indecisive Paul (the world never had a chance to get to know John Paul I), this new pope seemed to radiate an energy that was truly God-given. His charming smile, his confident stride, his ability to communicate in half a dozen languages, and at fifty-eight, his relative youth—all these coalesced into the making of John Paul Superstar. He was a telegenic figure and, from the beginning, he demonstrated a contagious energy and verve that did wonders for the Church's institutional self-esteem. And he was everywhere. Paul, who began the age of papal air travel, had committed himself to attending the Conference of Latin American bishops in Puebla, Mexico. John Paul I had canceled the visit, perhaps sensing that such a trip would be too taxing to his frail constitution. But John Paul II put it back on the papal itinerary, and just three months after assuming the throne of Peter, he was winging across the Atlantic, his plane filled with bewildered staff and enraptured journalists, to meet the bishops.

This was his first international challenge as pope, and it was a tricky one. At that time, some members of the clergy in Latin America had become enamored of the so-called theology of liberation, which encouraged priests to join in political action, sometimes even violent protest, against unjust governments. As a priest and bishop, Wojtyla had had vast experience in dealing with a system of government that he considered illegitimate. But for anyone who assumed that because he was relatively young, with a sense of humor, and acted more informally than his predecessors, he must also be politically liberal, John Paul's first trip abroad was a sobering revelation. In unmistakable terms the pope told the Latin American bishops that it was their job to save souls, not become enmeshed in politics. Injustice should be combated, but not by taking sides. In this judgment, John Paul was clearly influenced by a circle of conservative advisers who would play key roles in his papacy. Among them was Joseph Cardinal Ratzinger, the brilliant theologian John Paul named to head the Congregation for the Doctrine of the Faith. Ratzinger, seven years the pope's junior, had first encountered Bishop Wojtyla at the Second Vatican Council, where their intellects, ages, and personal experiences made them natural allies. Ratzinger freely admits that he went to the Council full of liberal ideas and enthusiasm, but by the time John Paul II was elected, he was one of the driving forces behind the new conservatism that would come to define the Wojtyla papacy.

John Paul also wasted no time publishing a letter to all the priests of his Church, warning them that he would not be as willing as Paul had been to permit them to leave the priest-hood. The pope wrote: "Since the priesthood is given to us so that we can unceasingly serve others, after the example of Christ the Lord, the priesthood cannot be renounced because of the difficulties that we meet and the sacrifices asked of us. Like the apostles, we have left everything to follow Christ; therefore we must persevere beside him also through the cross."

❖ ❖ ❖

". . . I have not stopped being a Polish bishop."

He had a similar warning for theologians whom he believed were straying too far from officially accepted Church doctrine. The occasion for John Paul's first salvo in his battle against doctrinal dissent was his first encyclical, *Redemptor Hominis* (Redeemer of Mankind). He reminded theologians that they have a special responsibility not simply to state their views; but also to serve the Church when they do so. The pope wrote: "Theologians and all men of learning in the Church are today called to unite faith with learning and wisdom, in order to help them to combine with each other. . . ." To many scholars who had been at odds with the Vatican in the past, the message was as clear as it was chilling. Perhaps inevitably, John Paul made one exception to his rule about not crossing the line into poli-tics: Poland. A few days after his election, he told Cardinal Wyszynski, the Polish primate: "I have become the bishop of Rome, but I have not stopped being a Polish bishop." So when the Vatican announced that the pope would visit his homeland in June 1979, there was considerable anticipation: How would he be welcomed by the Communist authorities with whom he had dueled as a bishop and cardinal?

That very question was being pondered by Edward Gierek, the first secretary of the Polish Communist Party, who knew that the people of Poland were bursting with excitement and pride over Wojtyla's election. Gierek also knew that the Kremlin, under the waning, unimaginative command of Soviet Communist Party leader Leonid Brezhnev, was concerned that a Polish pope would prove troublesome. In the end, Gierek opted for the high road, and with some notable exceptions of censorship, allowed Poland's people to celebrate the triumphant return of the native son. It was a calculated risk, and in all probability, it was the first major step on the road to the dismantling of the Soviet empire.

To say that Poland gloried in John Paul's arrival is an understatement. From the moment he knelt on the tarmac of Warsaw's Okecie Airport to kiss the soil—a ritual he would follow each time he visited a country as pope for the first time—the constraints of communism and Catholicism were lifted. The country let loose with nine days of mass gatherings that produced massive crowds: 300,000 for an open-air Mass in Warsaw's Victory Square; 500,000 in Gniezno, the ancient capital and seat of the Church in Poland.

His official speeches were studies in restraint, but the Poles who heard him—about one third of the country's population is estimated to have seen him in person during the trip—instinctively understood the meanings buried beneath the lines of text. His message to them, in the more than fifty addresses he gave, was essentially the same each time: Put your faith in God, and the suffering you now endure will someday be lifted from you. It was a homily of hope to a nation that, since World War II, had exchanged one occupation force for another and

saw no end in sight. As he had when he was a bishop and cardinal, John Paul managed to convey, between the lines, his
personal vision that communism was not an eternal force but
merely a passing aberration. Just as he wanted his Latin
American bishops and priests to do, he did not take sides and
preach revolution, but rather sowed hope.

The sight of a pope in the midst of an Iron Curtain country
exhorting the faithful to put their trust in God and wait for better days made the already heroic pope appear to be a political
and moral force unlike any other. In the United States, where
many people would not be able to distinguish Poland from
Bulgaria on a map of the world, this dynamic speaker and
valiant pastor seemed too good to be true. If he was willing to
take on the Communists, surely he could settle the ferment
that roiled within the American Church as a result of the Second Vatican Council. When it was announced that he would
come in September 1979 to New York and speak before the
United Nations, America prepared itself for a visitation unlike
anything since the Beatles.

He came, he was seen, but whether he conquered is a matter
of interpretation. John Paul accepted all the trimmings of
American adulation—a ticker-tape parade in New York, a
delirious sellout crowd for his Mass at Shea Stadium, and the
kind of media events at which he excels. This was his moment
to show Americans what he thought of them and their society.
He told them, all right, even if he did disguise it in his remarks
before the United Nations on October 2, 1979. "Disturbing factors are frequently present in the form of the frightful dispari-
ties between excessively rich individuals and groups on the one
hand, and on the other hand the majority made up of the poor,
or indeed, of the destitute, who lack food and opportunities for
work and education and are in great numbers condemned to

The pope at St. Patrick's Cathedral, New York City, 1979.

hunger and disease. It is no secret that the abyss separating the minority of the excessively rich from the multitude of the destitute is a very grave symptom in the life of any society."

What kind of talk was this? To American ears it sounded

downright leftist, maybe even socialist. This was the beginning of American recognition of the enigma that was John Paul II. Devoted anti-Communist that he was, at the same time he criticized harshly the injustices that resulted from unchecked capitalism. His call for a third way between those two systems was nothing new: He had seen its roots in the worker-priest experiments of France and Belgium that he visited in 1946 and 1947, and had spoken of the excesses of all political systems during his *A Sign of Contradiction* sermons to Paul VI.

Moreover, John Paul showed no sympathy to American notions of modernization when they involved innovations such as the end of priestly celibacy, or the ordination of women as priests. The pope received an unpleasant shock—and a valuable lesson on the American penchant for exercising democracy—when he spoke to a group of priests and nuns in Washington, D.C. There, Sister Theresa Kane, the head of the Leadership Conference of American Religious, bluntly accused him of insensitivity to the problems faced by women. She said: "As women we have heard the powerful messages of our Church addressing the dignity and reverence for all persons. As women we have pondered upon these words. Our contemplation leads us to state that the Church in its struggle to be faithful to its call for reverence and dignity for all persons must respond by providing the possibility of women being included in all the ministries of our Church."

John Paul heard her out in frigid silence and did not respond. It was clear he was not used to being addressed in this way. The smiling pope with the twinkling eyes also had limited tolerance for dissent.

Throughout his papacy, John Paul would view America— and it, him—with an admixture of admiration, puzzlement, and fury. To the pontiff who cries out for and insists on respect for human dignity, the sleek and sleazy pursuit of sex, drugs, and fast money that regulates part of American culture was not merely disappointing but also un-Christian. How, he asked, can a nation blessed with so much bounty be so unaware of the suffering of its own poorest and those of other lands? How can its citizens permit abortion—which John Paul, a survivor of the Nazis, considers nothing less than outright murder of innocents—while worrying over the ethics of wearing animal furs? He found baffling the obsession of American Catholics with issues such as ordination of women, homosexuality, and the celibacy of priests, when so many lack even basic understanding of their Church's teachings on matters of salvation. He regularly said "God Bless America" with the utmost sincerity when visiting the United States, but that does not mean that he would allow himself to be bound by its customs.

❧ ❧ ❧

"You cannot take a vote on the truth."

It is the peculiar lot of American Catholics to live in a functioning democracy, but to be members of a Church that is an absolute monarchy. Critics who excoriate John Paul as inflexible and unresponsive miss the point. The pope understands the freedoms that attend democratic institutions, but does not feel compelled to respond to their demands as would a president. Asked once if he would ever consider changing the bans on artificial contraception, or any of the other above points, John Paul told an American journalist: "You cannot take a vote on the truth."

If John Paul was disheartened by the response his message received in North America, he found an entirely different reception when he traveled to Africa, a continent where he envisioned a major role for Catholicism in the closing years of the century. In May 1980 he made an eleven-day tour—his longest time thus far away from the Vatican—to Zaire, the Congo Republic, Kenya, Ghana, Upper Volta (now Burkina Faso), and the Ivory Coast. The pope would spend an inordinate amount of time in Africa because he viewed it as a major opportunity for the Church to expand its spiritual borders beyond established areas of influence in Europe and the Americas. And this expression of concern by the new and charismatic pope met with great enthusiasm. The crowds he attracted were huge even by the standards of that huge continent. In Kinshasa, Zaire, people jostling to see him were trampled to death. In Kisangani, Zaire, the pope was infected by the enthusiasm of the dancing crowds and began to sway his own hips, with papal dignity but human enjoyment, too. The performance was impressive enough to lead one African bishop, Francis Arinze of Nigeria, to proclaim that a new age of Christianization had opened on the Dark Continent. In 1985 John Paul made Arinze a cardinal.

Though the pope resisted stoutly the philosophy of liberation theology that he saw springing up in Latin America, he was aware of the need to let far-flung Church institutions adapt to local customs. Thus it was on this trip that he unveiled publicly his carefully calibrated plan for permitting inculturation. The term refers to the mixture of traditional Roman Catholicism with native practices drawn from the African heritage of animism, a belief in the existence of spirits in objects other than the human being. One kind of local custom he did not intend to sanction was the common practice of priests living with mistresses and sometimes fathering children. Even as he watched local tribal dances, sometimes performed by bare-breasted women, the pope gave no ground on the issue of priestly celibacy. He told one crowd: "Your Church has been grafted onto the great tree of the Church, where for a hundred years it has drawn its sap, which now permits it to give its fruits to the Church and to become itself missionary to others. Your Church will have to deepen its local African dimension without ever forgetting its universal dimension."

The pope's exhausting foray into Africa was only the first of more than half a dozen he would take to the continent he called "ripe for harvest." And his calculations about its potential for adding to the rolls of the Church proved, as usual, accurate. Thoughout the 1980s, Catholicism grew at a rate of about 5 percent a year in Africa. The shepherd was finding new sheep.

Throughout his travels and the lengthy workdays he spent at the Vatican, John Paul never lost sight of the country he still considered his home. Yet even he was unprepared for the shattering events that would overtake Poland in August 1980 and set in place the chain of events that eventually would topple the pope's Communist adversaries, not only in Warsaw but in Moscow as well.

❧ ❧ ❧

"A showdown was becoming inevitable."

As had often been the case in Poland, the precipitating factor was that most basic commodity: food. Protests and strikes over increased prices had broken out in July 1980.

This time, however, there was little fear that the Communist authorities would respond with bullets. Edward Gierek, the Polish party leader, had gotten his job after his predecessor made the mistake of using force to smother the last strike. Gierek, while not a liberal by any means, was sophisticated enough to realize that the popular demands could not be ignored indefinitely. When Brezhnev lectured him on his duties as a Communist, Gierek replied that he also had duties as a Polish patriot. A showdown was becoming inevitable.

Though John Paul said nothing publicly about the gathering storm, he made sure he was kept aware of every event in his homeland. Years later, Polish political activists confirmed that priests were carrying sensitive communications back and forth between Rome and the various flash points of Poland—some with private messages and support and advice from the pontiff, who, as he readily admitted, had never stopped being a Polish bishop.

The situation became even more critical in August 1980. In the Baltic Sea port of Gdansk, employees at the Lenin shipyard locked the factory gates behind them on August 14 and insisted they would neither leave nor do any work until their demands for political and economic reform were met. Such brazen behavior by citizens behind the Iron Curtain was simply unheard of. Many expected a volley of gunfire to be the official reply. But that myopic view failed to take into account Poland's singular cultural, historic, and religious development. No other country in the Soviet orbit so straddled the border between East and West, between Christianity and Marxist atheism. No other member of the Warsaw Pact defense organization had such a bitter history of antagonism with Russia. And nowhere else in Eastern Europe but Poland was a full 95 percent of the population baptized Roman Catholic. The dynamics of the shipyard strike of 1980, it became clear, were more complicated than any challenge to Communist supremacy since the rise of the Bolsheviks in 1918.

History is written by the victors. Therefore it is impossible to know for sure what might have happened in Poland if a dark-eyed, mustachioed electrician and troublemaker named Lech Walesa had not scaled the fence of the Gdansk shipyard and joined his fellow workers inside. What is clear is that from that moment on, the strikers had a leader and the Western world a new darling. And it is hard to divine if Walesa, who at all times wore a pin with the image of the Black Madonna of Czestochowa in his lapel, would have had the courage to do what he did if he had not known that he had a friend and countryman watching over him from Rome.

Like millions of others, John Paul saw the enormous potential that the Polish workers' challenge offered to opponents of communism. Unlike many who hoped it would explode into outright warfare both to embarrass the Soviets and to test their resolve, the former cardinal of Kraków did not want political progress to cost lives.

The negotiations between the strikers—whose number had grown to include miners in Silesia—and the government included many demands, but the most important and, from the authorities' point of view, threatening one, was the insistence on a new trade union that was free of government domination. The Gierek regime was bargaining in good faith, but probably undercut its position fatally by making clear that it would not use force to resolve the impasse. It was perhaps the central factor that resulted in the nearly unbelievable events of August 31—an agreement between a Communist government and an independent trade union that clearly was not inclined to share the principles of socialism. The workers' success at budging the government in Warsaw, and by implication the one in Moscow, meant that Father, Bishop, and Cardinal Wojtyla had been right: The mastery of communism was temporary, and when challenged with sufficient force and moral suasion, could be made to yield. While the Poles celebrated their dramatic step toward political pluralism, John Paul savored the moment quietly, and continued to work in his singular way toward a far more difficult and elusive goal.

The publication of the pope's second encyclical, *Dives in Misericordia*, in November 1980 caused less comment than the first, *Redemptor Hominis*, but it was in some ways more revealing of Wojtyla's sober thinking about the state of the world. In it he wrote, "The present-day mentality, perhaps more than that of people in the past, seems opposed to a God of mercy, and in fact tends to exclude from life and to remove from the human heart the very idea of mercy. The word and concept of mercy seems to cause uneasiness in man, who, thanks to the enormous development of science and technology, never before known in history, has become the master of the earth and has subdued and dominated it." This was the Karol Wojtyla of Wadowice, the gentle, hopeful soul whose life was a model of enduring adversity and relying on God to see him through. It took little imagination to put the high-minded words into concrete terms of obedience and submission when he wrote, "The Church, having before her eyes the picture of the generation to which we belong, shares the uneasiness of so many of the people of our time. Moreover, one cannot fail to be worried by the decline of so many fundamental values, which constitute an unquestionable good not only for Christian morality but simply for human morality."

This was John Paul at his simplest, most direct, and most universal. He was not speaking only to Catholics, nor only to Christians, but to his fellow citizens, to all men and women

May 13, 1981: Mehmet Ali Agca attempts to assassinate John Paul II.

who believed that things were not going well in the world and that something had to change.

When he spoke in this way, the pope had an audience unlike that of any other human. While not everyone agreed with all he said, and while many of his own flock simply ignored his dictates on questions of morality such as abortion and birth control, John Paul used the Throne of Peter to maximum effect. The simple honor he seemed to represent encompassed the highest aspirations of mankind, its better side, its saintly self. His frequent foreign trips and his habit of visiting one of Rome's parishes—in working-class neighborhoods as well as its great cathedrals—each Sunday to celebrate Mass became as much a part of his persona as his angry insistence that world leaders respect human rights, as much as the spiritual succor he provided to his beloved Poland during the early days of its brave revolt against communism. He was a unique figure of authority and morality, a lightning rod of attention both for those who viewed him as the answer to the ills of the twentieth century and those who wanted to silence him forever.

❧ ❧ ❧

"Why did they do it?"

It was not just on foreign visits that the pope came in contact with large crowds. Each Wednesday afternoon he would make a solemn circuit of St. Peter's Square in Vatican City to bless the crowds from around the world who came to see him. To cover the maximum amount of ground and to see as many people as possible, the pope moved through the square aboard a white, jeeplike vehicle—dubbed the "popemobile"—that had been designed to allow him to stand, bracing himself with one hand, while he waved to the throng.

Mehmet Ali Agca, arrived early at the twenty-acre expanse of St. Peter's Square on Wednesday, May 13, 1981. The spring heat had calmed to a comfortable sixty-seven degrees by 5 P.M. when the roofless popemobile entered the circular expanse from the Arch of Bells side of St. Peter's Basilica and made a slow circle through the cheering crowd of some fifteen thousand. On his second lap, the pope, accompanied as always by Monsignor Stanislaw Dziwisz, his personal secretary, was leaning out of the vehicle to touch the hand of a little girl dressed in white. He was a perfectly posed target.

Agca fired three shots, hitting the pope with two of the bullets. One shattered his left ring finger and grazed his right arm. The other, more serious wound ripped through his stomach, missing his pancreas and aorta by centimeters. The third bullet missed the pope but managed to wound two American women in the St. Peter's Square throng.

His face contorted in agony, John Paul stood for a moment and looked at his right hand, which was already slick with his own blood, seeping through his white robes. He slumped down into the backseat of his car and looked with bewilderment at Dziwisz. The head of the Vatican security police threw himself over the wounded pontiff and ordered the driver to zigzag through the square, to make the pope a harder target for any more shots. Once away from the heavy concentration of people, the popemobile made its way to the Gemelli Clinic. Because of Rome's clogged traffic, the emergency sprint took twenty minutes. As the patient was wheeled into the emergency entrance, an eerie echo reverberated through the hospital's halls: "It's the pope, it's the pope." Still conscious and writhing in pain, the pope nevertheless managed to thank the attendants at the hospital; then, in his flawless Italian, asked the question the entire world wanted answered that day: "Why did they do it?"

Agca tried to flee but was captured almost immediately by a Vatican plainclothes policeman. His quick capture may have saved his life; despite the crowd's devotion to the Church and its leader, a few bystanders wanted to administer summary justice to the gunman.

Karol Wojtyla should have died. By all the medical accounts given of his wounds, he had no business surviving. But he did. Not only did he survive, but also, within five days, the sixty-one-year-old pope told a St. Peter's audience, via a recording, that he wanted his assailant to be forgiven.

This pope who had lived the life of a student, a laborer, an actor, and an intellectual now demonstrated a quality of charity that many believed was nothing short of saintly.

John Paul had wanted his third encyclical, *Laborem Exercens* (Human Work), to be published on May 15, 1981, the ninetieth anniversary of Pope Leo XIII's landmark work, *Rerum*

Novarum, which decried the changes that industrialization had brought to the workplace and warned that man's central role as a means of production was being endangered. The assassination attempt two days before meant that the encylical could not be released until September 14 of that year, a fact John Paul wryly noted in his dedication of the work.

It was a time of immense struggle for the working class around the world: In the United States, Ronald Reagan had just taken office as president and was in the process of breaking a strike by the air traffic controllers, a showdown that would weaken the face of American labor for years to come. In England, Margaret Thatcher had subdued the socialist coal miners' union and set the stage for a decade of her conservative rule. In the Communist bloc, matters were strained to the breaking point. The Soviet Union would fail to meet its harvest target for wheat, forcing it to import grain from capitalist powers. And in John Paul's native Poland, the Solidarity trade union movement was calling dozens of strikes and insisting on a share of decision-making power.

This was not a pope—nor a writer, for that matter—to split the difference, or to couch his opinions in nonpartisan platitudes. As pope, Wojtyla made the same appeal he had as a cardinal, for a third way between capitalism and communism. Clearly Wojtyla during his lifetime had experienced and rejected communism and felt little compulsion to dredge over its faults. He did, however, repeat the message he had sent in New York a year earlier, that he was concerned about the lack of dignity that capitalism provided to workers in the age of modernization: "Presupposing that different sorts of work that people do can have greater or lesser objective value, let us try nevertheless to show that each sort is judged above all by the measure of the dignity of the subject of the work, that is to say

❖ MEHMET ALI AGCA ❖

He was a combination of moron and madman, religious zealot and godless travesty, right- and left-wing radical. Mehmet Ali Agca, the Turk who shot and nearly killed John Paul II on May 13, 1981, had vowed to do so, yet was able to slip into St. Peter's Square on that gentle spring afternoon and discharge a Browning 9mm pistol at the pontiff's flowing white robes. Years later, his exact motivation was still unclear.

Born in a small Turkish town three hundred miles from Ankara and raised alone by his mother, Agca was a rowdy youth. In college, where he studied economics and literature, he gravitated to assorted political causes, and was arrested along with other suspected terrorists in 1979. While in custody, he admitted to the assassination of a prominent leftist Turkish journalist, and was on trial in October of that year when a group of military men sympathetic to Agca's nationalist philosophy helped him escape.

While he was at large, Agca wrote an audacious letter to the newspaper whose editor he claimed to have murdered, warning that if John Paul's scheduled November 1979 visit to Turkey took place, "I will kill the pope." Agca's threatening letter revealed his warped sense of political and geographic paranoia. Russian imperialists, he wrote, were sending the pope as their agent to Turkey in an attempt to prevent that Islamic country from becoming close to other Muslim lands in the Middle East. He referred to the pope as the "commander of the crusades" and said his assassination would be a response to the attack earlier in the year on the grand mosque in Mecca, which he insisted was the work of the United States and Israel, even though the incident was generally acknowledged to be the work of Islamic radicals. John Paul's visit to Turkey went ahead as planned, without incident. Meanwhile, the man who had implicated Agca in the killing of the editor was gunned down, probably by Agca himself.

Agca slipped out of Turkey to Iran and from there made his way to Germany. Later, it would be charged that he had been in the employ of, and his travels financed by, the Bulgarian secret service, which thought killing John Paul would please its masters in the Kremlin (that theory was never proven conclusively, and three Bulgarian diplomats charged with complicity in the assassination attempt were subsequently acquitted).

After the shooting in St. Peter's Square, Agca's movements in Europe were meticulously chronicled to see what, if any, aid he had received. He visited Vienna, Zurich, and Milan, and was implicated in the killing of two Turks in what was then West Germany during the time he spent there. In Milan, a Turkish woman thought she recognized the escaped killer near the city's famed cathedral and called police. By the time they arrived, the man was gone. He practiced traveling to Rome by rail on at least three occasions between April and May 1981. He even used a forged passport to enroll in a language school and take a brief vacation in Palma de Mallorca.

Carrying the Browning along with more than $400 in Italian and Swiss currency. Agca checked into the down-at-the-heels Pensione Isa near the Vatican on Sunday, May 10, 1981. He occupied himself by writing a foaming tract, discovered by the police after his arrest, in which he boasted, "I have killed the pope," and repeated his earlier ravings about a Russian and American conspiracy to keep Turkey from its Islamic destiny.

During a three-day trial, Agca admitted his guilt and was sentenced to life behind bars (Italy has no death penalty). Over the years, spent in Rome's Rebibbia Prison, he has variously claimed that he was Jesus Christ, the devil, and innocent. Two years after the attempt on his life, John Paul visited Agca in his prison cell and forgave him.

the person, the individual who carries it out. . . . In fact, in the final analysis it is always man who is the purpose of the work, whatever work it is that is done by man—even if the common scale of values rates it as the merest service, as the most monotonous, even the most alienating work."

Laborem Exercens is also notable for the emphasis that John Paul put on the then burgeoning phenomenon in the Western world of two-income families and the effect that working women would have on society. While recognizing that both economic need and women's increasing independence made this trend inevitable, the pope offered a cogent warning that since only women can be mothers, and since mothers have historically held families together, care must be taken not to break this vital link. "It will redound to the credit of society to make it possible for a mother—without inhibiting her freedom, with psychological or practical discrimination, and without penalizing her as compared with other women—to devote herself to taking care of her children and educating them in accordance with their needs, which vary with age. Having to abandon these tasks in order to take up paid work outside the home is wrong from the point of view of the good of society and of the family when it contradicts or hinders these primary goals of the mission of a mother. The true advancement of women requires that labor should be structured in such a way that women do not have to pay for their advancement by abandoning what is specific to them and at the expense of the family, in which women as mothers have an irreplaceable role."

That sentiment could have come from a feminist manifesto as easily as a papal document and indeed sounds more like a progressive battle cry than the ramblings of the aging misogynist John Paul was so often accused of being. As usual, his defense of women's dignity was overlooked in the West, where the only litmus test of women's rights was—and continues to be—sanctioning abortion on demand. The pope was playing a different tune, but few who did not know him recognized the melody.

Even while he was recuperating from his wounds, the pope was willing to make difficult decisions he knew would affect the Church for generations to come. One of the clearest indications of how he viewed the world was his decapitation of the Society of Jesus, the worldwide priestly order commonly known as the Jesuits. For centuries, the Jesuits had been the most influential missionary arm of the Catholic Church, taking its message to far-off corners of the earth. As it developed in power, however, the society also began to stray from the tested line of theology that was the hallmark of Catholicism.

Jesuits, for example, were involved in the theology of liberation movement that swept through Latin America before John Paul blunted its influence during the Puebla conference of 1979. Among them was Ernesto Cardenal Martinez, who had accepted the post as minister of culture in Nicaragua shortly after the victory of the Marxist Sandinista Party. Some Jesuits were also known to support radical ideas such as an end to priestly celibacy or an end to the Church's condemnation of artificial birth control. The Jesuits' liberal reputation was accompanied by outstanding accomplishments in academic as well as theological circles, but it was seriously at odds with the Polish pope's bedrock conservatism.

So when the Jesuits' superior general, Pedro Arrupe, suffered a debilitating stroke in August 1981, the pope, even while convalescing in the hospital, seized the opportunity to bring the society to heel. He installed a conservative Italian, Paolo Dezza, as its acting head, shocking those Jesuits who had grown accustomed to acting independently of Rome and signaling that this was a pope who would brook no dissent from his master plan. The pope was a loving father to all, but he could also be a stern one, as the Jesuits learned.

The pope could have been forgiven for wanting 1981 to come to a quick conclusion, but one more test of will awaited him, even as he struggled to recover from his shooting wounds. In Poland, Solidarity, under Lech Walesa's enthusiastic if not always measured guidance, had become a virtual second government. Hundreds of branches of the union had been formed in large cities and rural villages. Indeed, there was even a rural Solidarity to accompany the more established industrial union. Though Walesa had met with the pope and pronounced himself a fervent Catholic, the two men were markedly different in both their political styles and their agendas. Walesa seemed willing at some points to wager the country's fate on his ability to deal manfully with its Communist leaders. Solidarity had demanded a national referendum on whether the Communists should continue to govern in Poland, a proposal so obviously unacceptable to the Warsaw regime that even Walesa's supporters wondered if he knew what he was doing. The union also called for a national strike on December 17, to mark the Gdansk food riots eleven years earlier. From his hospital bed, and later from his summer residence in Castelgandolfo, John Paul monitored events with great caution and trepidation. His experience as a bishop and cardinal had taught him that dealing with Poland's homegrown surrogate leaders and its real masters in Moscow was a thing best handled by the coolest of heads. While he had no alternative but to encourage Walesa, the union leader's boldness worried him.

His concern was justified. In the early morning hours of Sunday, December 13, Polish Army tanks encircled Warsaw while thousands of Polish Army troops rounded up some fifty thousand of their countrymen. Walesa himself was roused from his home in Gdansk at 3 A.M. and taken to the capital, where he was held incommunicado. The Catholic Church hierarchy protested against the use of military terror to bring the country under control, but the words sounded hollow, especially in the absence of Cardinal Wyszynski, who was no longer alive when the country most needed his strength.

Apart from the presence of gun-toting troops in the streets, the most unnerving aspect in the early days of martial law was the cutoff of international telephone and telex services, suspension of all commercial flights, the sealing of the country's borders, the shutdown of movie theaters and schools, and the 10 P.M. to 6 A.M. curfew. Poles had grown used to discussing their country's events with each other and with their relatives all over the world. By effectively silencing them, the government, perhaps unwittingly, perhaps by design, robbed citizens of the ability to reassure each other that things would get better, and left them in a constant state of anxiety.

From Italy, John Paul felt particularly cut off from his beloved homeland. He gathered what information he could from diplomats and others who could get out of Poland, and dispatched his secretary of state, Agostino Cardinal Casaroli, to Washington, D.C., to discuss the situation with President Reagan. The American leader's lack of response to the crackdown was perhaps puzzling to the Vatican, given Reagan's strident comments about the Soviet Union during his first year in office. The United States and its allies had been prepared to react aggressively if Soviet troops stormed Poland, but by using only Polish soldiers, Prime Minister Wojciech Jaruzelski, a Polish Army general, had robbed the West of the opportunity to prove conclusively that the crackdown was at the behest of the Kremlin. In fact, the White House concluded that to move too

JARUZELSKI AND HIS PREDECESSORS

WOJCIECH JARUZELSKI ANNOUNCES THE ESTABLISHMENT OF MARTIAL LAW, 1981

The world reacted with shock when Wojciech Jaruzelski, grim-faced, and clad in a general's uniform, was named the leader of the Polish United Workers' Party in October 1981. His eyes hidden from the world by the tinted glasses he wore because of an old infection, Jaruzelski looked like the epitome of a Communist *apparatchik*. In truth, he was a passionate Polish patriot, whose agonizing decision to impose martial law saved his country from destruction by the Soviet Union.

The position to which he was elevated was not entirely enviable. His four predecessors over the three past decades had employed various degrees of repression and relaxation to keep Poland within the Soviet fold. Boleslaw Bierut had taken a hard line with the Catholic Church, imprisoning Primate Stefan Wyszynski and being excommunicated from the Church as a result. Wladyslaw Gomulka, who had become a hero of the country when he faced down Nikita Khrushchev in 1956 during the "Polish October," had later gone in the other direction, authorizing troops to fire on Polish rioters in Gdansk in 1970.

Edward Gierek came to power that year after the bloody response to the workers' rebellion and remembered the lesson imparted to him by the unfortunate Gomulka. While Moscow demanded explanations about how this Pole could have reached such a position, Gierek emphasized the fact that a son of the Polish nation had received a great honor. Of course, Gierek was anything but pleased by the results of the conclave, but rightly concluded that since there was nothing he could do about it, he should make the best of the situation. When the new pope expressed a desire to return to his motherland, Gierek and the other members of the Politburo once again pasted on smiles and welcomed him home. This decision was made against the advice of Soviet leader Brezhnev, who tried to convince Gierek to put off the pope's visit on the specious grounds that the entire Polish leadership was ill.

Gierek understood the importance of keeping relations open with the Catholic Church, especially with Wojtyla at its helm. Gierek had met with Pope Paul VI, and stayed in touch with Wyszynski throughout the turbulent days when the nascent trade union Solidarity began demanding more of a role in national decision making.

Gierek's skills as a political conciliator finally failed him in September 1980. At a Politburo meeting he did not attend—supposedly because of ill health—he was ousted as first secretary and replaced by Stanislaw Kania, a squat former blackmith known mainly within party circles for his utter lack of a sense of humor. Kania's selection was due more to his complete devotion to Communist orthdoxy than to his intelligence or resourcefulness.

This was the era of Solidarity's incredible growth, against all odds, into the organization that would test the limits of Soviet communism. With constant coaching from Moscow and with the world's attention focused on his country, Kania proved himself unsuitable for the task. Just a little more than a year later, in October 1981, the Politburo met again and handed the top party job to Jaruzelski, who was already prime minister and defense minister.

Although he looked like a military martinet to much of the rest of the world, Jaruzelski was a thoughtful, intense man who loved his country. During World War II he joined a remnant of the Polish Army that fought for his homeland's liberation throughout the war. That same love of Poland led him, as defense minister, to twice refuse to use troops to crush demonstrations during 1976. "Polish soldiers will never fire on Polish workers," he said, and true to his word, they did not during his tenure.

Yet as he watched Poland sliding downward into political chaos, he knew that the restive Soviet Union would not stand by quietly. In December 1981, faced with the near certainty of a Soviet invasion if he could not stop the wave of strikes, Jaruzelski saw martial law as the only way to save Poland. During the tense months that followed, Jaruzelski remained in touch with John Paul II through emissaries, and, as the Soviet empire began to collapse, was a key conduit through which the pope sent messages to Soviet leader Mikhail Gorbachev.

hastily and forcefully could create support for Jaruzelski as a patriot who was handling his country's domestic problems as he saw fit.

The pope at this point had to make a strategic decision, one that would, in one way, define his papacy. Would he continue to be a frontline Polish patriot, as he had been all his life? The possibility that he would go to Poland and stand with his countrymen in the days after martial law, was, according to some who knew him, very real. Or would be be a world figure, the Vicar of Christ to all the countries of the world, a leader who transcended geographical boundaries? This was the decision with which Wojtyla wrestled.

In the end, he did both. Through the secret written correspondence he maintained with Prime Minister Jaruzelski, the pope was able to learn what the regime in Warsaw was thinking and to understand what motivated its actions. The pope came to understand that to the men who were running Poland, the imposition of martial law was in effect a patriotic decision, one that had been made to prevent an even greater calamity—a full-scale invasion by Soviet troops. That was a real possibility, as both Jaruzelski and the pope realized. Soviet leader Leonid Brezhnev had sent members of the Politburo to Warsaw to warn the Poles in no uncertain terms that he would not allow the Solidarity union to become a full partner in running Poland. Even the small concessions that the union had won—open elections to represent workers, bargaining over working conditions and food prices, and two-way discussions about the direction the national economy should take—had infuriated the aged Soviet chief.

Both the pope and Jaruzelski knew that Soviet intervention would be a tragedy from which Poland might never recover. Unlike the Reagan administration, which at times seemed to be daring Moscow to take military action so it could retaliate, the pope above all wanted to spare his homeland from destruction. It was this, rather than any latent sympathy for the Communists, that dictated John Paul's cautiously prudent course of action in the weeks and months after martial law had been imposed. Through his back-channel communications with Jaruzelski, the pope developed a healthy respect for the general and recognized that, to him, curtailing basic freedoms with the use of Polish troops was an alternative infinitely preferable to having the same thing happen at the hands of Soviet intruders.

❧ ❧ ❧

"He has captured them completely."

As the months dragged on and it became obvious that Poland would neither be liberated from martial law nor explode into open civil war, John Paul was able to turn his attention—in public, at least—to other parts of the world. There was no shortage of crises. In May 1982 Argentina and Great Britain went to war over a fistful of windswept South Atlantic islands known to Argentineans as Las Malvinas and to Britons as the Falklands. The pope, who had been scheduled to visit Great Britain, was thrown into a quandary: Could he accept the hospitality of one of the combatants without offending the other? Specifically, could the head of the Roman Catholic Church be seen shaking hands with the leaders of a country whose people were 90 percent Protestant, while its troops fought forces from Argentina, with an overwhelmingly Catholic population? The pope used his incalculable reserve of energy and initiative to find a way around the problem: He conducted a wildly successful tour of the British Isles from May 28 to June 2, during which he met with Queen Elizabeth, the archbishop of Canterbury, and hundreds of thousands of Britons, most of them non-Catholic. To point out that his visit was not intended to signal political support for the British war effort, John Paul canceled a meeting with Prime Minister Margaret Thatcher. The pope, the first ever to set foot on British soil, had a simple message: We are all Christians; let us act that way.

The tactic worked with the British people. As one Catholic archbi shop put it: "He has captured them completely." To John Paul it was merely another tour in which he demonstrated his amazing personal charisma.

But the tour de force in Britain was only half the job. Just a week later, the papal plane was winging its way toward Argentina. John Paul had rightly calculated that to dispel any notion that he was in sympathy with Britain in the Falklands war, he needed to visit Argentina speedily. The pontiff knew that he could not afford to offend Latin America in this delicate moment if his long-term plan for promoting the Church in the Third World was ever to take root. Thus, when his jetliner touched down at Buenos Aires's international airport, the visitor from Rome had the same warm greetings for his hosts as he had demonstrated a week earlier in Britain. One Argentinean bishop was so taken in by the former actor's benevolence that he remarked: "The pope visited England as a duty. He comes to us because of love."

Whatever they thought, John Paul wanted both sides in the conflict to understand his opposition to it. "Join your hands in a chain of union that is stronger than a chain of war," he insisted during a Mass at Buenos Aires's Palermo Park. It was

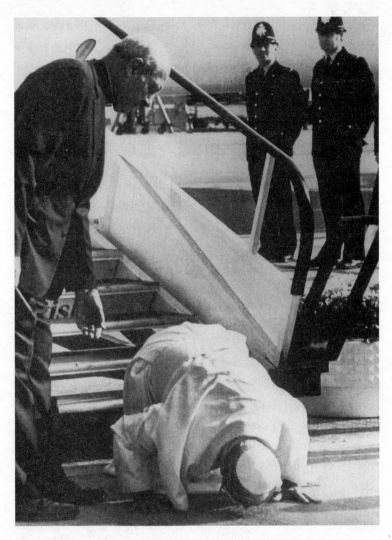

John Paul II kisses the ground as he takes his first steps in a new country, Great Britain, 1982.

too late to prevent bloodshed, as the pope knew, but he was not about to allow his message of peace to be drowned out by the sounds of gunfire.

After his exhausting journeys to Britain and Argentina, John Paul returned to Rome not depleted, but rather with a new determination to make his vision of a unified world and a unified Church into a reality. In this mission he was aided by the man with whom by now he had forged a deep intellectual and spiritual bond: Joseph Cardinal Ratzinger. Late in 1981 John Paul had summoned Ratzinger from Munich, where he was archbishop, to head the all-important Congregation for the Doctrine of the Faith. It was a job that few men could fill at all, let alone to the satisfaction of the Polish philosopher-pope, but Ratzinger was truly up to the task.

❖ ❖ ❖

"I was a progressive, really."

Ratzinger's life story bore an uncanny mirror-image relationship to Wojtyla's. As a sixteen-year-old during World War II, he was called up to service in the Nazis' paramilitary corps but was never involved in hostilities. Nevertheless, he saw some Jews—Hungarians, he believes—being loaded onto cars for transport to Dachau. In an interview in 1993, Ratzinger recalled those last days. "I could see all the problems of our country and of the world. I could see how destructive was atheism, the official government ideology. Only the Christian faith had the possibility to heal this people and give a new beginning." A German colleague in the Vatican is more blunt: "For a man like him to see such chaos was very distressing. He correctly foresaw that those demonstrations were a taste of the disruptions to come in the future. And if you look around the world now, what do we see? Uncertainty everywhere, questions, always questions, and after carefully thought-out answers are given, denunciations of the answers."

Ratzinger decided to be one of those who would show the way. He was ordained in 1951 and immediately showed vast promise as a theologian. His skill at intepreting doctrinal truth is based on his ability to synthesize vast amounts of material into clear, straightforward language that, characteristically, leaves no room for discussion or dissent. It was at Vatican II, where he served as an adviser to Joseph Cardinal Frings of Cologne, that Ratzinger met his Polish colleague for the first time. They were both relatively young men with budding reputations; both were eager to make their mark, within the confines of the Church. Thirty years later, recalling the heady days of the Council, Ratzinger said: "At that moment, we had great hope for the renewal of the Church, the liturgical movement, scriptural and ecumenical movements. And for us it was clear that a new scholastic system was also indispensable not only in the development of the Church, but now we are in a more open moment, we have the possibility to dialogue with the world and with non-Catholics, and we must open the ways for this development. I was following the ideas of Pope John, convinced that this was a providential moment, and we must do everything possible to give space to these new dimensions. And so, in that sense, I was a progressive, really."

It was not a mood that would last his whole life. In 1968 Ratzinger was the dean of theology at the University of Tübingen when students there, as in other halls of learning, began demonstrating for more academic and intellectual freedom. Ratzinger, the self-described progressive of the past, was horrified that theological students would question the existing order of authority. His students from that era recall that the effect on

Ratzinger was dramatic. He became a believer in applying the rules of the past to the conditions of the present—and Joseph Ratzinger, the future guardian of discipline for the Roman Catholic Church, had been born. In the 1993 interview Ratzinger reflected on his reputation for severity: "The Holy See is not a tyrannical institution, but it is also an institution of obedience. In a mutual obedience and a mutual process of learning, it is giving voice also to the people's desire to be really near Our Lord. I think often the Holy See is seen only as a very severe keeper of precepts and prohibitions: always against, always with burdens for the people. Yet every day in St. Peter's Square, I meet persons who are thankful that they have a voice, that they can touch the presence of the Church, that they can see that this is reality, that the reality continues. That gives us security in our faith. We have a way. God speaks with us."

For Ratzinger, truth is absolute, not relative. It is perhaps that certainty that makes him such a natural ally for John Paul, who, like his German brother, believes that even in the days of confusion that mark the end of the twentieth century, the absolutism of faith is not only desirable but also essential.

The keeper of the faith lives in an apartment just above an important bus terminus outside the Vatican. Each day he ambles across the cobblestones of St. Peter's Square, nodding to other clerics, stopping occasionally to chat with tourists. He insists that whatever papers he will be working with that day be waiting for him when he arrives at his office in the congregation. By mid-afternoon he is ready to return home, almost always with a briefcase full of work. But first he practices the piano for a quarter hour or so. He concentrates on Beethoven and Mozart. Brahms, he says disarmingly, is too difficult for him.

Ratzinger and the pope worked out a ritual of meeting each Friday at 6:30 P.M. for a discussion that generally lasted an hour, on theological issues. The German and the Pole—each of whom experienced World War II as youths, though from opposite sides of the battlefield—carry with them the scars of memory and the longing for order. They seldom disagreed on any major question. As one of Ratzinger's aides said in 1993: "They have come to the same conclusions by traveling different paths."

With Ratzinger at his side, John Paul was ready to take on the threats to the Church's authority that he saw developing in the world. First among these was the phenomenon of liberation theology, particularly in Latin America. Although he had spoken forcefully against this trend during his first foreign visit as pontiff, John Paul recognized the injustices that liberation theology was trying to address. His eight-day trip to Central America in March 1983 was, he told the vast crowds he encountered, designed to "share the pain" of the region's population.

It would have been impossible for the pope to omit Nicaragua from his itinerary, though he probably wished he could have. The Sandinista National Liberation Front (FSLN), which had seized power there in 1979, was openly Marxist, antireligious, and in no mood for lectures from a Polish pope who had already made known his feelings about liberation theology. Almost from the moment he touched down at Augusto Cesar Sandino Airport in Managua, he found himself in the unaccustomed position of being treated with intentional disrespect. He stood unprotected, under a wilting sun, as Sandinista leader Daniel Ortega Saavedra rattled off a nearly half-hour welcoming speech that stressed politics more than spirituality. Ortega made a special point of emphasizing that Catholics were among the leading supporters of the Sandinista revolution. By this he meant not just rank-and-file believers but also priests, including Miguel D'Escoto Brockmann, a Maryknoll priest who served as foreign minister, and the Jesuit Ernesto Cardenal Martinez, the minister of culture. Confronted with such an obvious challenge, John Paul decided to show that he, too, could play power politics. D'Escoto was out of the country (an unheard-of snub from any other foreign minister during a papal trip), but Cardenal, dressed in open-necked shirt and work pants, was midway through the airport receiving line that John Paul had to work. Perhaps realizing that he was in for a lecture, Cardenal pulled off his black beret, knelt before the pope, and tried to kiss his ring. John Paul was having none of it. Withholding his hands, he wagged both his index fingers at Cardenal and said severely, "You must regularize your position with the Church." The priest-minister, struck dumb with shock and embarrassment, could only nod his head in submission.

Later, at Mass in Managua's Plaza 19 de Julio, the pontiff was interrupted repeatedly by Sandinista youths chanting revolutionary slogans. Exasperated beyond tolerance, John Paul boomed "¡Silencio!" into his microphone, causing a temporary stunned quiet. From that moment on, the visitor from Rome made no effort to engage in diplomatic niceties with his Sandinista hosts. This was a pope who could respond in kind to the impieties of Communist *apparatchiks*. Thirteen years later, the pope would return to a post-Sandinista Nicaragua ruled by a fervent Catholic, Violeta Chamorro, and be swept up in its adulation. As was so often the case during his papacy, when he confronted antagonistic regimes, he had the final word.

The pope's 1983 mission to Central America was intended as a message of solidarity with the region's suffering masses. That it became instead a curtain that separated him from the political turmoil roiling there was not altogether his fault. Like Ratzinger, who advised him throughout on how to deal with the threat of priests caught up in leftist politics, John Paul recoiled from the messy chaos he witnessed in the Church, and took refuge in the calm traditions in which he had spent his adult life. He felt that the Sandinistas were little more than proxies for the Soviet Union, and he distrusted them instinctively. Likewise, the militant qualities of liberation theology were doomed to fail with him, since he read into that philosophy the rabid strains of socialism and state control. For all his intellectual qualities and worldly wisdom, this pope was still a man named Wojtyla, a man from Poland. And it was to Poland, his homeland still under martial law, that he returned, in June 1983.

❖ ❖ ❖

"Solidarity"

It was a far different homecoming from the pope's first Polish pilgrimage in 1979. On the plane from Rome, the pope was asked what he felt like. "Myself," he replied with that characteristic combination of humor and philosophy that marks his public persona. The man once known as Karol Wojtyla knew that, whatever personal joy he derived from seeing Poland again, this would not be a pleasurable experience. In December 1982 the prime minister and party leader, General Jaruzelski, had suspended the so-called state of war declared against his own country, but some of its strictures still applied.

His first meeting with the general, at the government's Belwedere Palace in Warsaw, was stiff and formal. Facing each other but separated by several feet and two microphones, the two leaders spoke directly to one another while ministers and clerics hovered around the periphery of the red-carpeted room. Jaruzelski alluded heavily to the fact that martial law, for all its inconvenience, had spared Poland from a far worse fate—a likely invasion by Soviet troops. John Paul listened carefully to the soldier-politician, then offered his own carefully wrought address in which he made plain that nothing but a return to open dialogue with the Solidarity trade union would be acceptable. For an instant after the speeches were finished the two Poles stared, each taking the other's measure. They both knew: There would be no breakthroughs on this trip.

That said, the pope enjoyed himself tremendously during the week he spent among his countrymen, and gave the Communists unending misery. He punned unremittingly on the word "solidarity," using it to indicate his oneness with other Poles, when everyone understood perfectly well he was offering heartfelt support for the still banned union.

If the homecoming in 1979 had been an unrestrained celebration of joy, the 1983 trip to Poland provided the kind of comfort that close friends offer each other during difficult moments. The pope's mere presence told Poles that they and their plight were not forgotten. In return, the total if noisy adoration he received from his countrymen gave John Paul a psychological lift he had needed badly since the assassination attempt.

In Poznan, in Katowice, in Czestochowa, and in Wroclaw, as well as in the capital, Warsaw, and his beloved home of Kraków, John Paul found himself a messenger of hope in a time of melancholy. After his appearances in each of those cities, revved-up crowds would spar with the nervous and overzealous riot police known as ZOMO. Sometimes taunts would be all that were launched; sometimes the exchanges involved stones and tear gas canisters. More than anything, the pope's presence provided the people of Poland with a sense of protection against a government they detested. As he had done in the 1979 visit, John Paul promised his listeners that the division of Europe into East and West, capitalism and communism, free and oppressed, was not necessarily permanent.

Though most Poles did not know about it until it had happened, the highlight of this papal trip was the pope's secret meeting with Lech Walesa, the founder of the Solidarity union. Though the union leader had been released from detention with the suspension of martial law, the regime decided it was less risky to let him meet the pope than to take the chance that John Paul would complain publicly about being denied such a visit. The gamble paid off. Though neither Walesa (who would go on to become president of Poland in 1991) nor the pope has confirmed it, it seems obvious in retrospect that the pope's message to him was to cool it. The Vatican's concern was that Poles not be slaughtered and the country turned into a battleground. Solidarity should not engage the regime on an aggressive basis. Instead, it should insist, peacefully, on a return to its pre-martial law status. The pope's seemingly conciliatory blueprint of action disappointed Solidarity activitists, who had hoped he would lead a battle cry. But the former actor from Kraków had to look at the entire world as his stage now, and consider with utmost care the impact of each of the lines he spoke. He left Poles unfulfilled in their desire for liberation, but happier for his presence, albeit brief.

❧　❧　❧

"It is I who am the pope."

With the situation in his homeland static for the moment, John Paul moved to shore up the Church administration, a sore

In Czestochowa, Poland, home of the Black Madonna, 1979.

point both for him and for the entrenched Italian cardinals who had come to think of Vatican affairs as their, and not the pope's, responsibility. John Paul made sure that notion did not sink in during his administration. When a self-important aide corrected him on a point of Vatican ceremonial procedure, the pope wheeled on the cleric and said, "It is I who am the pope." He reached beyond the normal clique of Italians and other Europeans to stack his Curia. He named Bernardin Gantin of Benin to lead the Congregation of Bishops, ensuring that any senior members of his Church would have to pass the ideological scrutiny of the brilliant and conservative African. To safeguard his long-expressed position that family life should be part of a deeper relationship with God, the pope tapped Colombian Alfonso Lopez Trujillo to head the Pontifical Council for the Family. Lopez did not rely on personal charm to carry out his responsibilities. A 1994 visit to his office in Piazza San Calisto, in Rome's Trastevere district, took months to arrange. Once in the cardinal's presence, the visitor was quizzed amiably but insistently on his religious beliefs, his marital status, and number of children ("Only two? Pity.") before any questions about his views on the role of women in the world could be asked—at which point the cardinal rose, bestowed his blessing, and declared the interview completed.

In the United States he was responsible for naming three of the country's most influential cardinals—John O'Connor in New York, Joseph Bernardin in Chicago, and Bernard Law in Boston. Each man had become a pillar in the structure of orthodoxy that John Paul tried to reinstill in the American Church. The outspoken O'Connor, in particular, became vociferous in his defense of the rights of the unborn and in condemning promiscuous sexual conduct, including homosexuality, while still feeling empathy for victims of AIDS.

Bernardin, an intellectual and one of the Church's truly great thinkers, became the personification, and eventual hero, in one of the darker elements of modern-day Catholicism. Accused by a gay man of molesting him during his days in the diocese of Cincinnati, Bernardin patiently denied the charges, endured the intense scrutiny that followed their publication, and resolutely resisted gloating when his accuser, who was suffering from AIDS, finally retracted his statement.

These men, and the dozens of others John Paul installed as cardinals during his pontificate, shared the pope's moral absolutism—wrong is wrong, nothing can make it otherwise. In Africa, where he saw the greatest opportunity for massive growth of his flock; in comfortable, materialist Western Europe; and in impoverished and confused Latin America, the pope inserted surrogates for his unbending beliefs who toed his line and made clear that lay Catholics were expected to do the same.

This had an added benefit often overlooked by secular minds: Within the Vatican, major decisions are reached not simply by papal fiat but by slowly evolving consensus. John Paul had been dismayed, to say the least, by the opposition, albeit subtle, he had encountered in his first years on the Throne of Peter. His decision to become actively involved in resolving the problems of Poland, for instance, were met with sage counsel that as pope he had to be a world leader, not just a Polish patriot. His condemnation of liberation theology worried some Curia members who thought that accommodation was the best way to secure the Church's influence in the Third World. John Paul realized that he could not take on the rest of the world until he had put his own Church in order. His appointments of cardinals and bishops, overseen by Bernardin Cardinal Gantin, were criticized by many liberal theologians for their ideological uniformity. But that was exactly the point: John Paul was packing his hierarchy with first-rate but reliable minds. It was the maneuver of a wily politician, a description of himself he would never reject.

In 1983 he created 18 cardinals; in 1985 he created 28

more, bringing the College of Cardinals to an all-time high of 152 members. This solid body of support would become crucial for the pope, who, perhaps more than many world leaders who had to worry about reelection and crowd pleasing, had the luxury of focusing his attention on doing what he thought was right. Thus, in 1985, John Paul was aware that changes were taking place in his native half of Europe—the East, the Soviet bloc—that would alter the course of the rest of the twentieth century. The most visible indication of renovation was the election of Mikhail Gorbachev as general secretary of the Soviet Communist Party. Younger than any of his recent predecessors, more vigorous and brimming with ideas he was anxious to test, Gorbachev in many ways resembled Karol Wojtyla more than either of them might have enjoyed admitting.

It was not immediately apparent that Gorbachev would be the leader to first admit the flaws of, and then help dismantle the seemingly permanent edifice of communism in Russia. His Politburo was stocked with old-line holdovers from the Brezhnev era, much as John Paul's Curia had been. Gorbachev's foreign minister, Andrei Gromyko, was more than ever "grim Grom," the scowling face of the Kremlin to the outside world. The pope met with Gromyko in 1979 and again in 1985, and neither audience went well. After the first encounter, the pope was asked if he found his busy schedule tiring. "The most tiresome of all was the one yesterday," he quipped. It did not take long for curious reporters to figure out to whom he referred.

Yet the pope seemed to have had an instinctual feeling that Gromyko's new master in Moscow was of a different breed—someone with whom he could deal, albeit from afar. In 1985, however, the time was not yet right.

Instead, John Paul's Vatican undertook a quietly astonishing array of diplomatic activities around the world that would, in a manner never given full credit by his critics, bring the Church of Rome into the twentieth century and position it for a role in the next millennium. In 1982 the pontiff met with Yasir Arafat of the Palestine Liberation Organization, an encounter that, although billed as private, sparked fears that the Church was taking sides with the Muslim world against Israel. To counter that impression, he met afterward with leaders of the Anti-Defamation League and condemned anti-Semitism as it applied to Jews.

But that was only one slice of John Paul's broad-based plan of action. In the space of a year he established relations with Denmark, Norway, and Sweden; met and prayed with the archbishop of Canterbury, Robert Runcie, the head of the Anglican Church; received the United Kingdom's first ambassador to the Vatican since the sixteenth century; and came to new terms with Italy on the relationship between the Vatican city-state and the country that surrounds it. Since 1929, those relations had been governed by the Lateran Treaty, signed on behalf of Italy by Benito Mussolini. John Paul wanted a more modern document that codified the Church's role in what is essentially its host state.

By the end of 1984 the pope had denounced apartheid in South Africa, signaling clearly that the Catholic Church would not sanction racism. He did, however, meet with the South African head of state, despite the protests of Anglican archbishop Desmond Tutu, who would later win the Nobel Peace Prize.

He also welcomed the first ambassador from the United States, a mark of favor to the Reagan administration and the beginning of a working relationship that, while sometimes overstated, was always based on goodwill and respect.

But John Paul reserved his most amazing surprise of 1984 for two days after Christmas. Following a recent tradition of popes visiting prisons (one of Jesus' instructions to his disciples), John Paul not only chose to go to Rome's infamous Rebibbia Prison but also sought out its most notorious inmate—Mehmet Ali Agca, the Turk who had tried to kill him in St. Peter's Square. He entered Agca's cell without hesitation, and brought with him a camera crew from the Vatican television service to immortalize the event. Their conversation, conducted in Italian, was never fully revealed. But John Paul's emotions were, even for this gifted actor, stunningly human and real. At times the pope leaned forward, clutching Agca's upper arm as they spoke. His eyes clenched shut as if in pain (a grimace of concentration that Wojtyla often employs), the pope imparted forgiveness to his would-be killer. It was an act of charity that made him entirely credible when he demanded that his fellow Catholics, no matter how oppressed by their government or by other tormentors, find the grace to pardon their enemies.

The pope was surely working on his fourth encyclical, *Slavorum Apostoli*, (Apostles of the Slavs) before Gorbachev rose to power in Moscow. Nevertheless, it was the first significant work he released during the Gorbachev era, and its timing could not have been more apt. The encyclical recognizes Sts. Cyril and Methodius, who brought the gospel of Jesus to the lands of Eastern Europe, including Russia. By turning his attention—even in such a metaphorical way—toward the East, the pope signaled to Gorbachev that the Vatican took Russia, its leader, and its problems seriously. Only a few years later, Gorbachev would note that his respect for Wojtyla made it easier for him to bring the pope into his confidence as he unleashed the astonishing changes that would spell the end of the Soviet Union and ultimately cost Gorbachev his position of leadership. The Communist in Moscow and the president in Washington both knew that the pope in Rome was a player.

Sudan, 1993

CHAPTER EIGHT

THE FINAL YEARS

---◆---

Presidents measure their impact by years, by popularity polls, and above all by getting reelected. As an absolute monarch, John Paul faced no such tests of his effectiveness, but neither did he have a consistently reliable way to gauge the feelings of his flock. His more than seventy trips to foreign lands and the dozens of other pastoral visits could be counted on to produce enthusiastic, cheering audiences. But the smiles and shouts of "John Paul II, we love you" told only part of the story.

The decade of the 1980s saw some astounding changes in the way ordinary people lived their lives. Computers became the workhorses not only of universities and research centers; they also carried out many of the calculations that hitherto required human intelligence. Medical science sought to answer basic questions of human existence: Should life be prolonged? By how much? At what cost? Can and should conception be avoided artificially? Is abortion moral? Spy satellites orbiting hundreds of miles overhead took pictures of such clarity that it was nearly impossible to know with certainty that you were not being observed. Systems of war were refined so that instant destruction of a country, or the entire world, at any given moment was a real possibility. These developments could be lauded as progress or scorned as perversion, depending on one's point of view, but with one exception, no world figure seemed able to put the process of modernization into the context of spirituality.

John Paul II has not learned to use a computer. Thoughout his life he has written his sermons, encyclicals, and books in longhand, or dictated them to a secretary. Though a man of the twentieth century, his formative years were spent in the first half of the 1900s, and, like many in middle age and beyond, he was skeptical of the changes that made its second fifty years a disconcerting race with innovation. That attitude has influenced some of his most important decisions as pope and has inscribed on his papacy the triple legacies of caution, traditionalism, and moral inflexibility.

In May 1986 the pope published his fifth encyclical, *Dominum et Vivificantem* (Lord and Giver of Life), a treatise on the role the Holy Spirit plays in the lives of Christians. It is not John Paul's best writing. Rather, it is a dense and closely reasoned letter that makes a point lay Catholics may consider esoteric: that without the influence of the Holy Spirit, Christians cannot experience the whole truth of their redemption. "On the horizon of contemporary civilization—especially in the form that is most developed in the technical and scientific sense—the signs and symptoms of death have become particularly present and frequent. One has only to think of the arms race and of its inherent danger of nuclear self-destruction. . . . It is a question of problems that are not only economic but above all ethical. . . . The mystery of the Resurrection and of Pentecost is proclaimed and lived by the Church, which has inherited and which carries on the witness of the apostles. She is the perennial witness to the victory over death that revealed the power of the Holy Spirit, and determined his new coming, his new presence in people and in the world. At the same time, she proclaims him who gives life: the Spirit, the Giver of Life; she proclaims him and cooperates with him in giving life."

With the exception of theologians and those within the Church whose business it is to analyze and interpret papal declarations, the importance of *Dominum et Vivificantem* was largely overlooked. Along with *Redemptor Hominis* in 1979 and *Dives in Misericordia* the next year, it constitutes a trilogy of inspirational meditation about the Holy Trinity that John Paul considered vital to anyone concerned with salvation. *Redemptor Hominis*, his first encyclical, challenges Christians to model their lives on the example of Jesus, the Son of God. *Dives in Misericordia* is a message of reassurance, a promise that God, creator of all, is also a merciful Father to whom we can turn for comfort as well as justice. John Paul had thus fulfilled a goal that for him, at any rate, was one of the highlights of his life: to reveal to a population desperately seeking guidance the path to eternal truth. That these works were never accorded the attention he felt they were due may have been one factor that embittered him toward the modern world and its trappings.

Because, increasingly, John Paul Superstar became John Paul Superscold. Anger punctuated many of his homilies in the 1980s. During a September 1987 pastoral swing through the United States—his second as pope—John Paul laid it on the line for so-called cafeteria Catholics, among them some clergy,

With Mother Teresa, Calcutta, India, 1986.

who believed they could pick and choose which rules to obey
and which to ignore. "Dissent from Church doctrine remains
what it is: dissent. As such it may not be proposed or received
on an equal footing with the Church's authentic teaching."
Later, in Detroit, he railed against the gap in affluence that set
the United States apart from much of the planet. "Seeking to
satisfy the dreams of millions, you can become lost in a world
of fantasy. You may choose to close in on yourselves, enjoy the
fruits of your own form of progress, and try to forget about the
rest of the world. Or you may choose to live up to the responsibility that your own history and accomplishments place on
your shoulders."

Such testy demonstrations were accompanied by a steadfast—critics would say sullen—unwillingness to bend on issues of morality that obsessed Americans. John Paul said no to married or women priests, no to sex before marriage, no to contraception, no to compromise of any sort. He even suggested during his 1987 trip that Catholics who cannot or will not obey all aspects of the Magisterium—the church's power and right to teach—should refrain from receiving Holy Communion. For John Paul, the choice was simple: "You cannot take a vote on the truth."

Though he was the same man, the John Paul of the 1980s seemed to have little resemblance to the smiling, saving Pole who had taken the world by storm years earlier. His best efforts to proclaim the message of Christ were not gaining the kind of acceptance he had hoped, at least not in the materialistic Western world. Polls consistently showed that American Catholics approved of the legal right to abortion almost as solidly as non-Catholics. They also used artificial means of birth control as often as non-Catholics. The rest of the developed world ignored the pope, too. In Italy, the birthrate was the lowest in Europe, even as out-of-wedlock pregnancies came to be tolerated. In Germany, theologians openly questioned the Vatican's right to keep homosexuals, married men, and women out of the priesthood.

His seventh encyclical, *Sollicitudo Rei Socialis* (On Social Concerns), was an acid denunciation of the economic and political ideologies of both the Western world and its socialist competitors. As he had throughout his life, Wojtyla saw communism as the height of political hypocrisy, and capitalism as a brutal discriminator against the weak, who needed and deserved help. As it turned out, the Soviet-style communism he had spent much of his early life combating would crumble during his papacy with unexpected speed.

Mikhail Gorbachev knew he could not continue to engage in a costly arms race with the United States and at the same time preside over the Soviet empire throughout Eastern Europe, Central Asia, and the transcaucasian regions. In increasingly apparent steps, the Soviet leader was signaling by 1988 that he was willing to make political concessions that would have been unthinkable only a decade earlier. He began with Poland, where the Solidarity union was still technically outlawed. In July of that year Gorbachev visited Warsaw and gave his assent for the Polish government to re-legalize the union and allow it to compete in open elections the next year. Those elections became a rout, with Solidarity winning every one of the Parliament seats it was permitted to contest. Starkly confronted with the consequences of loosening his grip, Gorbachev made a decision of incalculable difficulty: He stood out of the way and let history take its course. The floodgates had opened. The inmates of Eastern Europe began to stream westward, aided by Hungary, which, in defiance of its treaty with other Warsaw Pact nations, opened its border with Austria and let East Germans, Czechs, and its own people cross to freedom.

The pope knew what was happening in his homeland, of course. But even he was surprised by the events of the next several months. Between the electoral victory of Solidarity in June 1989 and the end of the year, the Soviet bloc would disintegrate into little more than a painful memory. In November the Berlin wall, which had separated the traditional capital of all Germany, was pierced, and the city again became one. The Communist Party lost its grip in Hungary as it did in Czechoslovakia in November. In December Gorbachev visited the Vatican, the first time a Soviet leader had seen St. Peter's. Though the press photographers kept their lenses focused on Raisa Gorbachev's short red dress—a violation of just about every Vatican protocol, but one that was borne silently—the real importance of the day was almost beyond comprehension. Gorbachev promised to extend religious freedom to his countrymen and proposed establishing diplomatic relations with the Holy See, another epochal step that was accomplished in 1990. Gorbachev and the pope had been feeling each other out for months, each relying on reports from Polish president Jaruzelski, who acted as mediator between these two modern-day emperors. They found that they could trust each other and, moreover, that they liked one another. It was a strategic friendship built on mutual need.

On Christmas Day 1989 Nicolae Ceausescu, who had ruled Romania through twenty-four years of personal deification, corruption, and terror, was executed along with his equally hated wife, Elena, at an army camp outside Bucharest. As 1990 opened, the Baltic republics, which had been annexed by the Soviets after World War II, declared their independence one by one, as did the lands of the Caucasus.

For the pope, as for the rest of the world, the final six months of 1989 were a period of change so historic and deeply felt that it was difficult to react quickly enough. At just about the same time that Ceausescu was being tried, convicted, and shot, U.S. forces invaded the Central American nation of Panama to capture its leader, General Manuel Noriega, and haul him to prison in Florida for drug trafficking. On Christmas Eve in Panama, Noriega realized the immensity of the invasion force, drove to a Dairy Queen restaurant, and called the residence of the papal nuncio, Monsignor José Sebastian Laboa, demanding asylum. When Laboa demanded to know on what grounds, Noriega had a cagey answer prepared. At this moment, he told Laboa over the phone, the pope is preparing to celebrate Christmas Mass, when he'll preach

RETURN OF THE NATIVE SON

◆ ◆

Karol Wojtyla's visits to Poland after his election required a massive security operation by the authorities, who, while less than pleased to have him back in his native land, certainly did not want him to come to any harm. Every available policeman and security officer was detailed to the mass events, to which millions streamed. Lost among the sea of faces but never relinquishing his own steady gaze on the pope was Roman Holdys, a member of the Polish secret police, who was John Paul's human shield against danger.

Now a retired colonel, Holdys recollected the three times he protected John Paul. "I spent every waking moment with him," Holdys recalled at his vacation dacha outside Warsaw. "Every morning he would look at me and smile and ask me if I'd slept well, and I smiled back and said yes. The truth was, I'd slept maybe thirty minutes, maybe an hour, waiting for him to wake up, waiting and watching."

They were an odd couple, the pope and the policeman. The first night that Wojtyla spent in his beloved Kraków, crowds camped outside the bishop's residence singing traditional

WELCOMED BY EXCITED CROWDS IN WARSAW, THE POPE RETURNS TO POLAND JUNE 1979.

Polish songs of love for him. At 2 A.M. Wojtyla, unable to sleep for the noise outside, stomped grumpily outside his room and encountered Holdys, keeping watch outside. "What's the matter, Your Holiness?" Holdys asked. "Would you like me to tell them to be quiet? I promise you, if I tell them to, they'll shut up."

"And what would be the point of that?" asked the pope, half smiling, half annoyed.

The next day, Holdys recalls, the pope had to negotiate a throng of well-wishers who tossed flowers in his path. This was fine with the policeman, except, as he puts it, "I didn't really know if they were roses or hand grenades. I tried to look at everything they threw to make sure it wasn't smoking, but it was really impossible. I tried to catch as many of them as I could, and throw them back, away from the pope, and wound up with cuts all over my hands."

The colonel thinks he may have been selected for this odd honor because he had the same blood type as Wojtyla, though even years later, Holdys refused to divulge what type it was. "I was a living blood bank, walking right beside him. And I knew if for some reason he should be shot, or injured in any way, I would be strapped down next to him, giving him the last drop of blood in my body to keep him alive."

When it was announced that Wojtyla would return in 1983, Holdys was again tapped to be the chief bodyguard. When he landed at the airport, the pope—who never forgets a face—had barely reached the bottom of the airplane's disembarkation steps when his face lit up at the sight of Holdys. "My colonel," he said delightedly. "Will you be with me again during the whole trip."

It was during that trip that he flew by helicopter to a remote mountainside to meet with Lech Walesa, the interned Solidarity leader. Holdys, as always, was at his side, and realized the importance of the occasion. He asked the pope if he would like some refreshment. The pontiff asked what kind of drinks were aboard. Holdys recalls: "It just so happened we had fruit juice, mineral water, vodka, brandy. I asked the pope if he wanted a glass of brandy. He laughed and said, 'Well, if you had any moonshine—the kind I used to have when I was young—I'd have a glass.' I didn't know what to do. I said to him, 'Your Holiness, I can radio ahead and have a bottle waiting for you when we get there.' And he laughed again and said, 'No, it won't taste the same on the ground.'"

The only real scare Holdys had was during the 1983 trip, at a Mass the pope offered in Warsaw's Victory Square. A man penetrated the "zero zone," the ten-square-meter perimeter that Holdys had insisted be kept clear of anyone except the pope's personal retinue. The man apparently meant no harm. He had wandered innocently past several layers of security guards and was drifting toward the altar with nothing more sinister on his mind than getting a better view of the pope. Holdys snapped an order to an underling, who approached the man and gently guided him away. The pope never knew that Holdys had gripped his automatic weapon inside his jacket pocket and was ready on an instant's notice to loose a deadly volley of bullets to protect the visitor from Rome.

about Mary and Joseph looking for a place to stay in Bethlehem. How can you turn me away?

The ploy worked, and for the next two weeks, Noriega was a most unwelcome guest at the residence. With the cacophony of communism's collapse consuming his days, the pope did not spend as much personal time as he might have otherwise, overseeing Noriega's eventual surrender to the Americans. But he did make known his anger at the way in which U.S. troops ringed his envoy's residence and blasted it day and night with ear-splitting rock music. An aide to the pope confided that such tactics were counterproductive from the pontiff's point of view. The right to asylum must be respected, said the aide, even for Lucifer.

❖   ❖   ❖

". . . it seemed the horror was coming to an end . . ."

For John Paul, the dazzling and devastating events of the year should have been the culmination of a victory he had been anticipating since his youth. Instead, he quickly and presciently saw in the overthrow of communism the unleashing of long-pent-up hatred between various nationalities. He warned: "Conflicts between ethnic minorities can be rekindled and nationalistic feelings can be exacerbated." The pontiff's words were largely lost in the months of celebration that followed the collapse of the Soviet empire, but they were soon to be borne out by horrible reality, as Azerbaijanis and Armenians slaughtered each other, as Lithuanians fell before a hail of Russian bullets, and as the newly liberated components of Yugoslavia began the dance of death that would last for more than five years and leave hundreds of thousands dead. As one of the pope's closest aides lamented with sorrowful precision: "Just as it seemed that the horror was coming to an end, another chapter of misery was just beginning."

Would anyone have begrudged him a moment of gloating? Could anyone doubt that Karol Wojtyla, himself a former inmate of communism's political penitentiary, had played a key role in its demise? Yet John Paul, ever a man in a hurry, moved quickly past the most significant shift of power of the late twentieth century and threw himself into crusades that would occupy the final years of his life.

Not surprisingly for a universal pontiff, John Paul's concerns ran the spectrum from the sexual obsessions of American Catholics to issues of genocide in less enlightened lands, where human rights were measured not in court decisions but in loss

t the Alamo, San Antonio, Texas, 1987.

of life. As soon as the threat of communism as a force in Europe had receded, the Polish pope was warning against the inherent inequality and moral laxity that a sudden onrush of materialism would bring. Again, his words were drowned out in the initial euphoria of freedom. But within a few years, the wisdom of that warning was clear. Bulgaria, Slovakia, and even Poland installed candidates who espoused an updated version of socialism, largely in response to the economic uncertainty that capitalism had introduced. And across the eastern half of Europe, the excesses of unfettered freedom were being devoured. Prostitution, which officially did not exist under communism, became a frequent source of income for families unable to keep pace with the challenges of the free market. Pornography was sold in street kiosks in Warsaw, Budapest, even Wadowice, the pope's birthplace. Criminal organizations sprang up and made Eastern Europe a clearinghouse for drug trafficking from Turkey and the Middle East. South American cocaine cartels found a new and voracious market for their powder. A once unthinkable sight in Communist Europe became commonplace: Homeless people, many of them elderly, begged for alms and waited for death, wondering when their newfound freedom would translate into happiness.

John Paul visited Wadowice in August 1991, a sentimental journey that was at best bittersweet. Kneeling in the nave of the church where he had once been an altar boy, the head of the Universal and Apostolic Church warned once again that political and economic freedom required greater responsibility from those who enjoyed them. As his motorcade took him past the sights he had seen daily as a child, John Paul knew that his papacy was about to embark on its most difficult phase, one in which there were no right answers, only less wrong ones.

He faced an agonizing decision in the former Czechoslovakia, where the Communist regime's persecution of the Church had been especially intense. In response, Czech bishops had secretly ordained hundreds of underground priests who celebrated clandestine Masses, administered sacraments, and kept the flame of faith alive. But the bishops could not be choosy about whom they made priests. Many of them were married men, and in some cases, women. John Paul thus confronted the question of what to do with them. Were they, after all, clerics? If so, how could he continue to oppose the ordination of female and married priests throughout the rest of the world? Or were they ordained illicitly? In that case, the Church had been guilty of hypocrisy of the highest order. The pope took the path of least resistance. He recognized the ordinations as special cases and tried quietly to transfer most of the married and women priests to low-profile posts.

In overwhelmingly Catholic Ireland, he was confronted by treachery of the worst kind. Bishop Eamonn Casey of Galway was found to have fathered a child with an American woman, who eventually exposed him. Across the North Sea, the Church of England decided in 1992 to ordain women priests, a move the Vatican angrily decried as a serious obstacle to eventual unity between the denominations. In America there was a sudden upsurge in the number of Catholic priests who were either accused of or admitted to sexually molesting children. These sorts of scandals undermined the pope's ability to offer inspiring examples of faith to his flock and held the Church up to ridicule. The pope, said a Rome-based official, received news of such setbacks with a combination of righteous anger and humble acceptance. It was for him another dose of suffering to be endured on his path to heaven.

Another kind of affliction became public in 1992, when the

pope stunned a St. Peter's Square crowd by announcing that he would enter the Gemelli Clinic in Rome for removal of an intestinal obstruction. It would be the first time the pope had checked into the city's most famous hospital since being shot in 1981. This was a different kind of medical problem. It also involved a decidedly older and more fragile man. At seventy-two, John Paul suddenly seemed like a pope whose reign might be coming to an end.

As is often the case when personal and not spiritual matters are being discussed, the Vatican was less than forthcoming about the nature of the pope's condition. The obstruction turned out to be a precancerous tumor the size of an orange. It was removed, but the news that the pope's normally vigorous health was under assault began a spate of rumors. Some said the doctors who removed the tumor had found his insides riddled with advanced cancer and, faced with an impossible task, sewed him back up and kept quiet. Another published report said the pope had contracted a life-threatening disease through contaminated blood used during the operation to save his life after the assassination attempt. To all these suggestions, the Vatican maintained a dignified silence. Joaquin Navarro-Valls, the multitalented, multilingual Spaniard who served as the pope's official spokesman, used his credentials as a physician to assure the outside world that John Paul was in the best of health. From then on, the pontiff's physical condition was the stuff of speculation everywhere in Rome, from gritty taverns to glittering embassy receptions.

Despite, or perhaps because of the fact that his health was now being openly called into question, John Paul made 1993 a year of practically nonstop travel. Moreover, he chose to spend much of his time in lands where he saw the future of the Catholic Church to be the brightest. Africa, in particular, became a favorite papal destination. He had made ten trips to the continent by 1996, and seemed, paradoxically, to be more at ease there than when he was in developed countries. On one visit to the Congo in 1980, when "John Paul mania" was still in full swing, the pope slipped away from his security detail and joined in a native dance being performed by part of his welcoming committee. His cautious tolerance of inculturation—the practice of mingling animism, spirit worship, and other local traditions with the traditional Roman Mass—was challenged consistently by his Curia but slowly made progress toward acceptance. It is fair to ask why John Paul was willing to embrace African variants on traditional Catholicism while harshly condeming liberation theology in Latin America. The answer, put simply, is that he did not view inculturation as a direct challenge to his conservative political outlook.

By 1993 the Catholic Church saw Africa as the most fertile ground for evangelization. Christianity was struggling for influence with Islam, especially in northern Africa. In Sudan, for instance, the Islamic-dominated government had tried to impose *sharia*, the set of civil laws based on the teachings of the Koran, not only on Sudanese Muslims but also on the approximately 2 million Catholics who dwelled largely in the southern part of the country. The pope decided to confront the challenge directly. In Khartoum in February, during a speech he delivered with the country's leader, General Omar Hassan Bashir, sitting directly behind him, the pope insisted: "All the Church asks for is the freedom to pursue her religious and humanitarian mission. This freedom is her right, for it is everyone's duty, the duty of individuals and the state, to respect the conscience of every human being." The challenges to Christians continued in Sudan, but John Paul's no-nonsense approach marked him in African eyes as a man of courage.

". . . this man from Rome is a good man . . ."

Nowhere had human dignity been trampled so thoroughly as in Albania, during decades of misrule by its Stalinist strongman, Enver Hoxha. Like most of the rest of Eastern Europe, Albania writhed its way out of communism in 1990, but that transformation hardly solved all its problems. It was the poorest country in Europe, rife with corruption, massive unemployment, and few prospects that things would improve. While John Paul knew of the misery that Albania's Catholic minority was enduring, the trip was nevertheless, for him, one of celebration. The country's small Catholic enclave was concentrated not in the capital, Tirana, but in Shkoder, to the north. A modest cathedral had once stood there, but Hoxha, determined to wipe out any vestige of a deity except himself, had turned it into a gymnasium.

On April 25, 1993, John Paul made a one-day visit to the country to reconsecrate the cathedral and mark the rebirth of Catholicism in Albania. Tirana's two hotels were reserved for dignitaries, but the residents of the capital opened their homes as well as their hearts to visitors. One withered man who spoke no language but Albanian pointed out that he was the same age as the pope, though he (the man) looked a decade older. He was an atheist, he said, but wanted to see the pope before he died. "I know that this man from Rome is a good man," he said of the pontiff. "He has survived much evil, just as I have. I will believe whatever he says."

And so, on that day, the man from Rome walked slowly up the aisle of the freshly painted, newly blessed cathedral. His gait was not the usual vigorous one that had propelled him a distance greater than a trip to the moon and back. It was, rather, the stately progress of a man who felt his time coming to an end. Before he got to the main event—the ordination of four bishops to minister to Albania's Catholics—he sat heavily in a makeshift throne behind the altar and watched the approach of a row of shy young girls, each bearing some symbolic gift.

There are moments that remain fixed in the mind forever. As he watched the girls come toward him, Karol Wojtyla was transformed from a tired old man into the Vicar of Christ. The old Polish actor had thrived on the reaction and encouragement of crowds all his life. But on that April day in Albania, he demonstrated why he had been called to the Throne of Peter. Each little girl bowed or knelt before him as she presented her gift. And each one received the gift of a few seconds of undivided attention from the Successor of the Fisherman. John Paul hugged each child to him in the most loving, fatherly way imaginable. He had not mastered Albanian, but through his unfailing ability to communicate with anyone, the pope nodded to each child and smiled, then bestowed a hug, a kiss, and his apostolic blessing.

For John Paul, it was all in a day's work. He was back in his Vatican apartment by midnight. But through his presence for a few hours, and his genuine kindness to a handful of smiling little girls, he brought hope and happiness to a tortured land, and carried out, once again, his mission to spread the word of his God.

Toward the end of summer in 1993, John Paul was again airborne, this time winging toward the unlikely destination of Denver, Colorado, for the celebration of World Youth Day. He had instituted the custom of bringing the world's young people together to hear him in 1986. Just as he was convinced that the Third World, particularly Africa, offered the best hope for the Church's future, he realized that there was a burgeoning new generation—young men and women who might have been his grandchildren had his life taken another path—looking for the meaning of life. As he had demonstrated with the young girls in Albania, John Paul had a way with young people that bridged the gap between his severe outlook and rigid demands upon the world and their fresh-eyed optimism about their lives that lay ahead. In Denver, where hundreds of thousands of teens and twentysomethings had converged, the pope had decided to make one last stab at explaining to Americans why he could not put his stamp of approval on their hedonistic lifestyle.

He began with a blunt sermon to the nation's leader. John Paul had not met Bill Clinton before August 12, 1993, when his plane touched down at Stapleton International Airport. But the pope had already expressed his disapproval of Clinton's support for abortion rights. Further, he knew that the young president was struggling in his first year in office, and had come to Denver not just to welcome him officially, as protocol demanded, but also in the hope of catching some of the reflected rays of the pope's popularity.

Although the pope had just completed an exhausting itinerary in Jamaica and Mexico before coming to Denver, he was in fine form at the airport ceremony. Clinton's staff had not forwarded the president's speech to the pope, a normal courtesy for such a visit, so the pontiff was unsure what the president might say. To guard against surprises, the pope trusted once again to his own gift of stage presence. After several minutes of wild ovation from the crowd, the pope deadpanned: "You have really strong voices." The cheering started all over again.

"There is special joy in coming to America," John Paul said. "A nation that itself is still young according to historical standards"—and here he ad-libbed again—"what is two hundred years for a nation?" Once again, a raucous cheer went up, and again John Paul, twinkling with humor, said, ". . . really strong voices."

Clinton's remarks were standard fare, though he displeased the Vatican staff by specifically pointing out that in America, individual rights were paramount—a clear reference to his pro-choice position on abortion.

As the president and pope left the airport for a private meeting at a nearby college campus, one man was looking nervously from one camp to the other. Raymond Flynn, the former

The pope with President Clinton at World Youth Day in Denver, 1993.

Democratic mayor of Boston who was America's ambassador to the Vatican, had hoped this first meeting would be the beginning of a beautiful friendship. Instead it was already crumbling into a debacle.

Flynn had a vested interest in rescuing the relationship. A Clinton supporter, he had arrived in Rome with plans to turn the Vatican ambassadorship into a roving diplomatic troubleshooter post as well as the filter through which the pope's and president's interactions would pass. But it all depended on this meeting going smoothly. By the time the two principals emerged, word had spread through their respective camps: Soft-pedal the differences. Neither man wanted their embryonic ties to degenerate this quickly, though it was clear they would never have the kind of rapport that John Paul had enjoyed with Ronald Reagan and George Bush.

For the moment, though, the pope was concentrating his fire not on any individual, but on the messenger of the system he found intolerable. Speaking at McNichols Arena on August 14, the pope voiced his concern about the violence that made America an unsafe country. "Who is responsible?" John Paul asked. "Individuals have a responsibility for what is happening. Families have a responsibility. Society has a heavy responsibility. Everybody must be willing to accept their part of this responsibility, including the media. . . ." These last words drew a shriek of loud applause. Sensing he had touched on a crowd pleaser, the pope drew out the phrase again: "The mee-di-ya. . . ." Again, the hall went wild. John Paul paused for a second, perhaps decided whether to ad-lib or not, and deciding to take the risk. "So, the pope criticizes the media that put him on the television. . . ." The applause resumed, louder than ever. John Paul smiled, pleased with his own performance. Here, as in his first visit to the United States

fifteen years earlier, was the charismatic Polish pope
Americans loved to have among them.

❧ ❧ ❧

"*Because, man, he's the absolute neatest.*"

The high point of the Denver trip was a Mass the pope would
celebrate in Cherry Creek State Park, a vast expanse of field
and woods outside the city. For hours beforehand, kids from
around the world trooped up hills, carrying backpacks and
tents in which they spent the night. Not all the arrangements
would have pleased the visitor from Rome. One bearded boy
and his auburn-haired companion strode hand in hand toward
the makeshift altar. Why, they were asked, had they come to
see the pope?

"Because, man, he's the absolute neatest."

"So you like what he says?"

"Oh, yeah, I dig his message. He's all for loving each other
and not getting bogged down in hate."

"And what about the things he has to say regarding morality?"

"Yeah, morality. That's really important, too."

"Now, you two, are you married?"

"No, man."

"But you're lovers?"

"Well, sure."

"Are you aware that the pope says it is wrong for unmarried
people to engage in sex?"

The boy stared for a moment, as if to make sure his ques-
tioner was serious, then said: "Aw, you know, man, he's really

cool. He'd understand." And with that, they hurried off to see their hero.

That conversation summarized the basic disconnection between John Paul and the young people he wanted so much to bring into his orbit. They loved him, but felt no compunction to obey his instructions, especially those they found inconvenient. To John Paul, such lukewarm support was meaningless. Blind adoration without devotion to the deeper principle he was espousing was, he once told a friend, like talking about dinner without actually eating.

The pope was not about to sugarcoat his message at Denver. He wanted—here more than anywhere—to make this group of young people understand that while the world they would inherit was full of wonder, it was also fraught with danger. "With the passing of time, the threats to life do not lessen," he told them. "They grow enormous. There is spreading, too, an antilife mentality—an attitude of hostility to life in the womb and life in its last stages. Precisely when science and medicine are achieving a greater capacity to safeguard health and life, the threats against life are becoming more insidious. Abortion and euthanasia—the actual killing of another human being—are hailed as rights and solutions to problems. The slaughter of the innocents is no less sinful or devastating simply because it is done in a legal and scientific way. In the modern metropolis, life—God's first gift and the fundamental right or every individual on which all other rights are based—is often treated as just one more commodity to be organized, commercialized, and manipulated according to convenience."

Afterward, the pope's aides said he had worked dozens of hours on this presentation, making sure that his tone conveyed both the urgency and the passion he attached to this crusade for life. And perhaps his message reached a few of the hundreds of thousands who heard him preach. "John Paul Two, we love you!" they chanted, and seemed to mean it. The pope smiled back like a father who knows his children are good kids, but apt to misbehave, and answered: "John Paul Two, he loves you, too."

And then he left them to learn the lessons of life.

In Rome, there had been speculation for months—and within the courtyards of the Vatican palaces, for years—about the contents of John Paul's tenth encyclical. Everyone knew it would address the explosive issue of moral values. Everyone knew it would be the capstone of the pontiff's teaching. But how would he convince a skeptical, pleasure-seeking world to redirect its attention to the questions of salvation that had dominated his own life?

Veritatis Splendor (The Splendor of the Truth), his 179-page masterpiece, underwent dozens of rewrites and was signed by the pope on August 6, 1993, but was not released until October 5, 1993. For six years, he had labored on it, since first announcing his desire to put in writing his thoughts on the nature of, and difference between, good and evil. If that self-assigned task seemed useless, or obvious to some, it was not to a thinker of Wojtyla's profundity.

Are there degrees of evil? Is theft less a violation of God's law than murder? Can an action that is wrong in one century become less evil with the passage of time? Does one's conscience have the ultimate power to arbitrate between right and wrong?

While it is as much as work of literature as philosophy, John Paul's answers to these questions are unmistakably clear and contained in one word: No. Wrong is wrong and right is right, and no amount of justification can change that simple truth. "Today it seems necessary to reflect on the whole of the

Church's teaching, with the precise goal of recalling certain fundamental truths of Catholic doctrine that, in the present circumstances, risk being distorted or denied. In fact, a new situation has come about in the Christian community itself, which has experienced the spread of numerous doubts and objections of a human and psychological, social and cultural, religious, and even properly theological nature with regard to the Church's moral teachings."

Thoughout this deftly worded argument for individual restraint, John Paul refers to the modern-day tendency to make exceptions to rules based on convenience or circumstance. While news headlines focused on his specific mention of birth control, artificial insemination, euthanasia, and abortion (somehow implying that the pope might choose to use the encyclical that he considered a summation of his pontificate to reverse a lifetime of deeply held beliefs), the most interesting question posed in *Veritatis Splendor* is whether an individual's freedom to choose, to reason, and to consider an action must be taken into consideration when determining if a given action is right or wrong. The pope argues that freedom must be combined with morality if man is to avoid a constant state of chaos. Without an underpinning of morality, human actions cannot be judged on their effect, but only on the basis of our freedom to choose them.

He wrote: "All people must take great care not to allow themselves to be tainted by the attitude of the Pharisee, which would seek to eliminate awareness of one's own limits and one's own sin. In our own day this attitude is expressed particularly in the attempt to adapt the moral norm to one's own capacities and interests, and even in the rejection of the very idea of a norm." If anyone thought John Paul, late in life, might possibly relent on his rigid views of morality, *Veritatis*

Splendor put an end to it. Moral relativists launched the expected denunciations, but the Vatican ignored them, just as for decades John Paul the bishop, cardinal, and pope had sloughed off criticism of his leadership.

There was one last surprise left in the active year of 1993. On November 11, after receiving a group of employees of the United Nations at the Vatican, John Paul tripped on the hem of his robes while descending a set of steps. His shoulder was dislocated and he was told not to go skiing anymore. He meekly accepted the treatment his doctors prescribed, then guiltlessly disobeyed their orders by heading for the hills to partake of his favorite winter sport. Right was right and wrong was wrong, but for the pope, even in his seventies, skiing was more important than doctors.

Usually, John Paul made headlines by going somewhere outside of Rome to deliver his message of redemption. In 1994 he created news in his bathtub. The pope had just finished bathing on the night of April 28 when he slipped and broke his right femur. The injury was not life-threatening, but it hobbled the pope like nothing else since his brush with death in 1981. Confined first to a hospital and then to his apartment, the restive pontiff was forced to cancel most of his travel schedule in 1994, including a much anticipated trip to the United Nations and subsequently to the eastern United States. Hobbled by a cane that he never learned to use properly, and obviously in pain when he put weight on his reconstructed hip, the pope appeared to age dramatically in 1994. His slightly stooped posture became more exaggerated when he walked. His wry humor was less apparent, and his general audiences each Wednesday, when visitors from all over the world are invited to receive the papal blessing, seemed less like opportunities than ordeals for him.

His physical travails were accompanied by a series of confrontations in which John Paul stuck resolutely to deeply held, if unpopular viewpoints. Even before he left the Gemelli Clinic, where he once again took up temporary residence during his recovery from the fall, he issued an apostolic letter in which he ruled out, once and for all and with unconcealed impatience, the possibility of admitting women to the priesthood. Although he stopped one step short of invoking the claim of papal infallibility, the pope's language left no doubt that he wanted this debate concluded. "Ordination," he wrote, "which hands on the office entrusted by Christ to his apostles of teaching, sanctifying, and governing the faithful, has from the beginning always been reserved to men alone. In some places it is nonetheless considered still open to debate. Therefore, in order that all doubt may be removed regarding a matter of great importance, I declare that the Church has no authority whatsoever to confer priestly ordination on women, and this judgment is to be definitively held by all the Church's faithful."

In fact, the letter was little more than a restatement of the Church's long-standing policy. Like popes before him, John Paul was saying that women could not be priests, not because he did not want them to be, but because he did not possess the authority to admit them. It was not he, but the eternal head of the church, Jesus, who had chosen not to include women in the original priesthood, which was the band of twelve apostles. Revisionists later argued that Jesus has also not spoken about space travel or television, and yet both things are now accepted. But the pope, in his elevated way, counterargued that women did exist in the time of Christ and that He had therefore had a reason for not making them priests. It was another example of an agonizing issue that John Paul wished he could make disappear but that he knew would not. The wording of the letter

In the Dolomites, 1996.

appeared to bind future popes to John Paul's view on the subject. That, in turn, renewed speculation that the pope was preparing for the end of his reign and was trying to make sure that no successor could ever reverse his position.

By that time, John Paul recognized, perhaps with bitterness, perhaps with resignation, that he would never be able to convince the Western world, especially the United States and Europe, to put aside its agenda of equality and freedom and to replace it with one steeped in humility and human dignity. When the pope visited the United States in 1995, a year later

A DAY IN THE LIFE
OF THE POPE

Get up early if you plan to follow John Paul II all day. The pontiff awakens at 5:30 A.M., dresses unaided, and after a prayer in his apartment, is in his private chapel at 6:15 A.M. The chapel is spare, but contains a large crucifix overhanging the altar and a copy of the Black Madonna of Czestochowa, Poland's holiest icon. He says Mass here at 7 A.M., and attendance is a high honor, usually reserved for about fifty people the Pope himself has singled out.

REACHING OUT TO TOUCH A BABY, POPE JOHN PAUL II VISITS THE ST. MELCHIADE PARISH IN ROME, 1987.

At 8 A.M. he has breakfast, usually with half a dozen or so guests who are selected because they know something about a topic on which the pope has expressed interest. His eating habits vary, but at the first meal he usually has fruit, bread, and jam, washed down with tea.

At 9 A.M., breakfast finished, the pope goes to his study in the Vatican to write for an hour or two. At times he prostrates himself on the floor, as he did when he was a young priest.

By 11 A.M. the pope has begun his daily round of private audiences, which are exhausting for him but provide lifelong memories for each of those he sees. Official visitors such as heads of state are conducted to the pontiff's library or one of the Vatican's official rooms. Less formal visits may take place in the pope's living quarters. He sees between four hundred to five hundred visitors privately a year. During this time the pope also sees some of his highest-ranking Curia officials. Unlike other popes, John Paul established fixed times for each of his top aides to meet with and report to him. He established early in his pontificate an insistence that those to whom he grants time be fully prepared for any questions he may ask them. Each Wednesday is set aside for the general audience, when several hundred visitors from around the world will receive the papal blessing in the auditorium behind St. Peter's.

At about 1:30 P.M., the pope has a working lunch, with guests selected according to the topic that interests him. Often, while he is planning one of his four to five foreign trips a year, he will talk to the cardinal of the country he plans to visit, or to experts on the political, economic, or social situation there. Lunch on Wednesday is usually reserved for Camillo Cardinal Ruini, the vicar general of the Rome diocese, which the pope formally oversees. After lunch, the pope may take a bit of exercise in the Vatican gardens or on the terrace of the Apostolic Palace. Increasingly, that physical activity gives way to a few hours' rest. The only people who have unfettered access to him are his personal secretary, Monsignor Stanislaw Dziwisz, and his official spokesman, Joaquin Navarro-Valls.

By 4 P.M. the pope is back at his desk, writing or taking care of administrative chores. He usually prefers to work alone, but at times is aided by one of the Polish nuns who rotate as his private secretaries and take dictation or file the correspondence he has already handled.

He receives a second wave of visitors at about 6:30 P.M., usually Curia officials. His secretary of state, Angelo Cardinal Sodano, is summoned twice a week, as is the secretary for affairs of the Church.

Dinner usually begins at 7:30 P.M. The pope enjoys one or two glasses of white Italian wine with dinner, but his favorite beverage is tea. Guests at dinner tend to be friends, as opposed to the official or working visitors who crowd his lunch table. The pope eats sparingly, usually a plate of pasta followed by a Polish-style meat dish with cooked vegetables, and fruit for dessert. As often as not, he is carried away by whatever conversation he is having, and lets his food grow cold.

At 8:30 P.M., the pontiff returns to his study for yet another round of paperwork. It is during these evening hours that he functions best as CEO of the Church. Drafts of documents pass across his desk, and none can be published without his personal approval.

Once a week, John Paul goes to confession, and every day he recites the breviary, which is the duty of every Catholic priest.

At 11 P.M. the pope goes to his apartment for final prayers and sleep. He kneels for the last time each day in his private chapel and offers thanks to God on behalf of his flock of 1 billion people.

than originally planned, he made few attempts to charm the millions who turned out to listen to him in New York City, in New Jersey, and in Baltimore. When, during a rain-soaked mass at the Meadowlands, the crowd took up the familiar chant of "John Paul Two, we love you," the pope squinted for a long time while considering his response. "Maybe," he said at last.

In Berlin in 1996, his popemobile was stoned and splattered with tomatoes by rowdies who wanted him to reverse his position on birth control, abortion, ordination of women—in short, by those who would never accept his authority yet wanted to be called members of the family of Christ. Aged and infirm, John Paul bore the insults in silence, moved with dignity through his agenda, and returned, as always, to Rome, to the Vatican, to the place where he knew one day he would be buried.

Early in 1996 the pope released a document titled *On the Vacancy of the Apostolic See and the Election of the Roman Pontiff.* It sets out with the greatest precision the protocol to be followed when a pope dies. Minute details are spelled out, such as the duty of the College of Cardinals to destroy the dead pope's Fisherman's Ring, and the lead seal with which he endorsed official documents. The method of voting is also described in painstaking detail: Even in the age of computers, the election of a pope will take place on paper ballots, with the handwriting of the elector disguised and the ballot carefully folded twice.

Vatican aides pointed out that the creation of such a document is a sitting pope's duty, much like a final will and testament, and dismissed any suggestion that John Paul was making final preparations for his death. But it is hard to imagine the newly elected Karol Wojtyla, confident, vigorous, and possessed of that infectious smile, spending hours upon the construction of such a document. At age seventy-six, John Paul was getting ready to die.

Toward the end of his instructions, the pope adds a personal note to his successor, an oddly reassuring message that could come only from one who has mounted the Throne of Peter. "I ask the one who is elected not to refuse," John Paul writes, "for fear of its weight, the office to which he has been called, but to submit humbly to the design of the divine will. God, who imposes the burden, will sustain him with his hand, so that he will be able to bear it. In conferring the heavy task upon him, God will also help him to accomplish it, and in giving him the dignity, he will grant him the strength not to be overwhelmed by the weight of his office."

Officer's son, soccer goalie, aspiring actor, quarry laborer, friend of youth, earnest priest, prolific author and dramatist, piercing philosopher, effective bishop and cardinal, polyglot, crowd pleaser, superstar, Vicar of Christ, and future saint—of all the descriptions of Karol Wojtyla, the one he has preferred is the most humble: servant of the servants of God. There will be no pope like him again, for he is a man fashioned for the challenge of leadership during an age of mass murder and tyranny, of mind-boggling change and advance, and of conflict between individual rights and collective responsibililty. His reign as the 264th shepherd of the Universal and Apostolic Church, a line that began with St. Peter, has been a combination of modernization and standstill, of intense personal involvement in the affairs of humanity and resolute, sometimes chilling, intolerance of its foibles and failures. Karol Wojtyla was a man; John Paul has been more. He has been the link between mortals and their maker, the prophet sent to the desert known as Earth to give us strength, to show the way, to serve.

CHRONOLOGY

1920   May 18: Born in Wadowice, Poland
       June 20: Baptized
1929   Mother, Emilia Wojtyla, dies of heart and kidney
       failure
1930   Enters high school
       Makes a pilgrimage to Czestochowa to see the Black
       Madonna
1932   Brother, Edmund, dies of scarlet fever
1938   Meets Prince Adam Sapieha, Archbishop of Kraków
       Graduates from high school
       Moves to Kraków with his father to attend Jagiellonian
       University
1939   September 1: Nazi Germany invades Poland
1940   Summer: Takes a job at the Solvay chemical plant
1941   February 18: Father, Karol Sr., dies
       August 22: Forms the Rhapsodic Theater with friends
1942   October: Begins to study in secret for the priesthood
1945   January: Nazis pull out of Kraków
1946   November 1: Ordained a priest
       Mid-November: Moves to Rome to study at the Angelicum
1947   Summer: Travels to Marseilles to observe worker priests
       Jan Tyranowski, one of Wojtyla's first mentors, dies.
1949   Parish priest in Niegowici, Poland
       Parish priest at St. Florian's in Kraków
1951   Sapieha dies

1958	August: Nominated auxiliary bishop of Kraków
	Pope John XXIII announces the second Vatican Council
1962	October 11: The Second Vatican Council opens
1963	May: Meets Franz Cardinal Konig
	December: Nominated to be archbishop
1967	May: Named a cardinal by Pope Paul VI
1968	Student riots in Warsaw
	Publication of *Love and Responsibility*
	July: Encyclical *Humanae Vitae* (On Human Life) is released
1976	Food riots in Poland
1978	August 6: Pope Paul VI dies
	September: Pope John Paul I dies
	October 16: Karol Wojtyla elected
1979	Releases first encyclical, *Redemptor Hominis* (Redeemer of Mankind)
	June: Visits Poland for first time as pope
	September: First visit to U.S. as pope
1980	May: Makes an eleven-day tour of Africa
	August 14: Labor strike begins at Lenin shipyards in Gdansk, Poland
	August 31: Labor agreement reaches in shipyard strike
	November: *Dives in Misericordia* (Mercy's Wealth) released
1981	May 13: Severely wounded in assassination attempt by Mehmet Ali Agca
	September 14: Release of *Laborem Exercens* (Human Work)
	December 13: Martial law declared in Poland
	Summons John Cardinal Ratzinger to head Congregation for the Doctrine of the Faith

1983   March: Eight-day trip to Central America, including
        Nicaragua
        June: Second visit to Poland
1984   December 27: Visits Mehmet Ali Agca in prison
        Release of *Slavorum Apostli* (Apostles of the Slavs)
1986   May: *Dominum et Vivificantem* (Lord and Giver of Life)
1987   September: Second visit to the United States
        Release of *Sollicitudo Rei Socialis* (On Social
        Concerns)
1991   August: Visits Wadowice
1992   Has an intestinal obstruction removed at Gemelli
        Clinic
1993   October 5: Release of *Veritatis Splendor* (The Splendor
        of the Truth)
1994   April 28: Breaks his right femur
1995   Visits United States
1996   October: Has his appendix removed

BIBLIOGRAPHY

Balducci, Ernesto. *John, the Transitional Pope*. New York: McGraw Hill, 1964.

Bigongiari, Dino, ed. *The Political Ideas of St. Thomas Aquinas*. New York: Macmillan. 1953

Flannery, Austin, O. P., ed. *Vatican Council II, The Conciliar and Post Conciliar Documents*. Northport, N.Y.: Costello Publishing Company, Inc., 1975.

John XXIII. *Peace on Earth*. Vatican City: Libreria Editrice Vaticana, 1963.

John Paul II. *On the Dignity and Vocation of Women* (Mulieris Dignitatem). Vatican City: Libreria Editrice Vaticana, 1988.

———*The Splendor of the Truth* (Veritatis Splendor). Vatican City: Libreria Editrice Vaticana, 1993.

———*On the Holy Spirit in the Life of the Church and the World* (Dominum et Vivificantum). Vatican City: Libreria Editrice Vaticana, 1986.

———*The Role of the Christian Family in the Modern World* (Familiaris Consortium). Vatican City: Libreria Editrice Vaticana, 1981.

———*In Commemoration of the Eleventh Century of the Evangelizing Work of Sts. Cyril and Methodius* (Slavorum Apostoli). Vatican City: Libreria Editrice Vaticana, 1985.

———*Redemptor Hominis* (Redeemer of Mankind). Vatican City: Libreria Editrice Vaticana, 1979.

————*Laborem Exercens* (Human Work). Vatican City: Libreria Editrice Vaticana, 1981.

Johnson, Paul. *A History of Christianity*. New York: Atheneum, 1976.

————*Pope John Paul II and the Catholic Restoration*. New York: St. Martin's Press, 1981.

Kelly, J. N. D. *The Oxford Dictionary of Popes*. Oxford: Oxford University Press, 1986.

Macciocchi, Maria Antonietta. *Le Donne Secondo Wojtyla*. Milano: Edizioni Paoline, 1992.

McDermot, Timothy, ed. *Selected Philosophical Writings of Aquinas*. Oxford: Oxford University Press, 1993.

Malinski, Mieczyslaw. *Pope John Paul II: The Life of Karol Wojtyla*. New York: Seabury Press, 1979.

Melady, Thomas. *"The Ambassador's Story, The United States and the Vatican in World Affairs."* Huntingdon, IN: *Our Sunday Visitor*, 1994.

Neuner, J., and Dupuis, J. *"The Christian Faith in the Doctrinal Documents of the Catholic Church."* London: Collins Liturgical Publications, 1983.

Paul VI. *On Human Life* (Humane Vitae). Vatican City: Libreria Editrice Vaticana, 1968.

Ratzinger, Joseph Cardinal, and Messori, Vittorio. *The Ratzinger Report*. Leominster, MA: Fowler Wright Books Ltd., 1985.

Solo Per Amore. *Riflessioni sul celibato sacerdotale*. Milano: Edizioni Paoline, 1993.

Szulc, Tad. *John Paul II, The Biography*. New York: Scribner, 1995.

Walsh, Michael. *John Paul II, A Biography*. London: Harper, 1994.

Wojtyla, Karol. *The Collected Plays and Writings on Theater* (translated by Boleslaw Taborski). Berkeley, CA: University of California Press, 1987.

Wynn, Wilton. *Keepers of the Keys, John XXIII, Paul VI, and John Paul II: Three Who Changed the Church*. New York: Random House, 1988.

SOURCES

CHAPTER ONE
REFERENCES
Vatican Press Service; Szulc; Johnson.
INTERVIEWS
Father Malinski, Danuta Michalowska, Father Andrzej Bardecki, Father Suder, various residents of Wadowice.
SOURCES
Description of Wadowice, of Wojtyla apartment, and of church, based on the author's trips there between 1983–85 and 1994.

p. 10 *"Through the course of history"*: Vatican Press Service, 1979.

p. 15 *"He had every opportunity"*: author interview with Michalowska.

CHAPTER TWO
REFERENCES
Encyclopaedia Britannica; *Tysodnik Powszechny*; Szulc; Malinski.
INTERVIEWS
Malinski, Bardecki, Suder, Michalowska.
SOURCES
p. 27 *"The soul sings"*: St. John of the Cross, *Encyclopaedia Britannica*, vol. V, p. 587.

p. 28 *"He was renowned"*: author interview with Michalowska.

p. 30 *"I met Karol"*: ibid.

p. 30 *"What we did"*: ibid.

p. 31 *"This theater, in which"*: *Tysodnik Powszechny*, 1958 (translation).

p. 31 *"He's a man living"*: author interview with Michalowska.

p. 34 *"For him, the presence"*: author interview with Malinski.

CHAPTER THREE

REFERENCES

Bigongiari; Malinski; Szulc; *Encyclopaedia Britannica*; Walsh; Wojtyla, *Love and Responsibility*; Wynn.

INTERVIEWS

Malinski, Stefan Wilkanowicz, Marek Skwarnicki.

p. 40 *"goal and justification"*: Bigorgiari, p. 3.

p. 44 *"faith, morality"*: Quoted in Szulc, p. 168.

p. 48 *"I have two"*: Author interview with Bardecki.

CHAPTER FOUR

REFERENCES

Bigongiari; Flannery; *Conciliar Documents*; Balducci.

INTERVIEWS

Malinski, Wilkanowicz, Bardecki, Skwarnicki, Tadeusz Mazowiecki.

SOURCES

p. 55 *"To adapt more"*: Conciliar Documents

p. 59 *"It's not an easy book"*: Author interview with Bardecki.

p. 66 *"As bishop of Kraków"*: Author interview with Wilkanowicz.

p. 66 *"He used small group"*: ibid.

CHAPTER FIVE

REFERENCES

Szulc; Walsh; Wynn; Paul VI.

INTERVIEWS

Wilkanowicz, Suder, Bardecki, Malinski.

SOURCES

p. 70 *"He was not constrained"*: Author interview with Wilkanowicz.

p. 71 *"He had no premonition"*: Author interview with Suder.

p. 71 *"He wanted to spend"*: Author interview with Bardecki.

p. 74 *"We could not regard"*: Paul VI, *Humanae Vitae*, Libreria Editrice Vaticana, p. 8.

p. 75 *"Some people today"*: ibid, p. 16.

p. 75 *"Not much experience"*: ibid, p. 17.

p. 81 *"He went to Zakopane"*: Author interview with Malinski.

CHAPTER SIX
REFERENCES
Szulc; Walsh; Wynn; *Time*.
SOURCES
p. 92 *"I do not know"*: *Time*.

CHAPTER SEVEN
REFERENCES
John Paul II, *Redemptor Hominis*, *Dives in Misericordia*, *Laborem Exercens*; Johnson, *A History of Christianity*; Kelly; Walsh; U.S. Catholic Conference.
INTERVIEWS
Wilton Wynn, John Cardinal Ratzinger.
SOURCES
p. 97 *"Since the priesthood"*: *Letter to All Priests*, 1979, Libreria Editrice Vaticana, p. 12.

p. 97 *"Theologians and all men"*: *Redemptor Hominis*, 1979, Libreria Editrice Vaticana, p. 54.

p. 97 *"I have become the bishop"*: Walsh, p. 45.

p. 99 *"Disturbing factors"*: Text of speech, U.S. Catholic Conference.

p. 101 *"As women we have heard"*: Walsh, p. 66.

p. 102 *"You cannot take a vote on the truth."* The pope said this to Wilton Wynn, my predecessor as *Time* magazine bureau chief in Rome and one of the finest journalists ever to cover the Vatican. Wynn used the quote in his book, *Keepers of the Keys*, and repeated the story to me personally. It is used here with gratitude.

p. 104 *"Your church has been grafted"*: *Time*, May 12, 1980.

p. 107 *"The present-day mentality"*: *Dives in Misericordia*, 1980, p. 8.

p. 107 *"The Church, having before"*: ibid, p. 61.

p. 111 *"Presupposing that different"*: *Laborem Exercens*, p. 16.

p. 114 *"It will redound"*: ibid, p. 70.

p. 119 *"Polish soldiers will never"*: Reported in many sources.

p. 122 *"He has captured"*: *Time,*. June 7, 1982.

p. 122 *"The pope visited England"*: *Time*, June 21, 1982.

p. 122 *"Join your hands"*: ibid.

p. 124 *"I could see"*: Author interview with Ratzinger, 1993.

p. 124 *"For a man like"*: ibid.

p. 125 *"At that moment"*: ibid.

p. 126 *"The Holy See"*: ibid.

p. 127 *"They have come"*: ibid.

p. 128 *"You must regularize"*: *Time*.

p. 132 *"It is I who am the pope"*: Wynn, and author interviews.

p. 135 *"The most tiresome"*: Wynn, p. 66.

CHAPTER EIGHT
REFERENCES
John Paul II, *Dominum et Vivificantem*, *Veritatis Splendor*; *New York Times*; Szulc; Walsh; Wynn; *Catechism of the Catholic Church*.

SOURCES
p. 140 *"On the horizon"*: *Dominum et Vivificantem*.

p. 142 *"Dissent from Church doctrine"*: Author's personal observation.

p. 142 *"Seeking to satisfy"*: ibid.

p. 146 *"I spent every"* and ensuing: Author interview with Roman Holdys, 1994.

p. 148 *"Conflicts between ethnic"*: Author's observation.

p. 149 *"Just as it"*: Author's observation.

p. 153 *"All the Church asks"*: *New York Times*, February 8, 1993.

p. 154 *"I know this man"*: Author's personal observation.

p. 156 *"You have really"*: ibid.

p. 157 *"A nation which itself"*: ibid.

p. 158 *"Who is responsible"*: ibid.

p. 160 *"With the passing"*: ibid.

p. 161 *"Today it seems necessary"*: ibid.

p. 162 *"All people must take"*: *Veritatis Splendor*, p. 78.

p. 164 *"Ordination, which hands"*: On the Vacancy of the Apostolic See and the Election of the Roman Pontiff.

p. 169 *"I ask the one"*: ibid.

PHOTOGRAPHY CREDITS

pp. iv, 146 courtesy of AP/Wide World Photos

pp. 1, 52 © Joe Crachiola/FPG International

p. 2 courtesy of Laski/SIPA Press

pp. 3, 13 courtesy of Laski/SIPA Press

p. 5 courtesy of AP/Wide World Photos

p. 9 courtesy of Laski/SIPA Press

p. 20 courtesy of Laski/SIPA Press

pp. 21, 25 courtesy of Laski/SIPA Press

p. 32 courtesy of Laski/SIPA Press

p. 36 courtesy of Laski/SIPA Press

pp. 37, 49 courtesy of AP/Wide World Photos

p. 39 courtesy of AP/Wide World Photos

p. 46 courtesy of AP/Wide World Photos

pp. 53, 63 courtesy of AP/Wide World Photos

p. 60 courtesy of Archive Photos/David Lees

p. 65 courtesy of AP/Wide World Photos

p. 68 courtesy of AP/Wide World Photos

pp. 69, 77 courtesy of AP/Wide World Photos

p. 72 courtesy of AP/Wide World Photos

pp. 80, 85 courtesy of Laski/SIPA Press

p. 82 courtesy of Master /SIPA Press

p. 84 courtesy of AP/Wide World Photos

p. 91 © Elliott Erwitt/Magnum Photos, Inc.

p. 94 © Jean Gaumy/Magnum Photos, Inc.

pp. 95, 157 courtesy of UPI/SIPA Press

p. 100 © Burt Glinn/Magnum Photos, Inc.

p. 108 © Dolf Preisgke/Magnum Photos, Inc.

p. 112 courtesy of AP/Wide World Photos

p. 118 courtesy of AP/Wide World Photos

p. 123 courtesy of Archive Photos

p. 132 © Bruno Barbey/Magnum Photos, Inc.

p. 138 © Abbas/Magnum Photos, Inc.

pp. 139, 165 courtesy of AP/Wide World Photos/Vatican POOL

p. 142 © Raghu Rai/Magnum Photos, Inc.

p. 149 courtesy of AP/Wide World Photos

p. 166 courtesy of AP/Wide World Photos

INDEX

ABOUT THE AUTHOR

John Moody was formerly *Time*'s bureau chief at the Vatican in Rome, Italy, and New York. He is the co-author of *The Priest and the Policeman*, the true story of Father Jerzy Popieluszko, the chaplain of Solidarity who was murdered by the Polish secret police, and a novel, *Moscow Magician*, based on his experiences as UPI's correspondent in the Eastern bloc. He is currently a senior executive at Fox Network News.